PSYCHOLOGY
IN CHRISTIAN PERSPECTIVE

PSYCHOLOGY
IN CHRISTIAN
PERSPECTIVE

An Analysis of Key Issues

Harold W. Faw

foreword by **Ronald P. Philipchalk**

Baker Books

A Division of Baker Book House Co
Grand Rapids, Michigan 49516

© 1995 by Harold W. Faw

Published by Baker Books
a division of Baker Book House Company
P.O. Box 6287 Grand Rapids, MI 49516-6287

Printed in the United States of America

Library of Congress Cataloging-in-Publication Data

Faw, Harold W.
    Psychology in Christian perspective : an analysis of key issues / Harold W. Faw : foreword by Ronald P. Philipchalk.
      p. cm.
    Includes bibliographical references and index.
    ISBN 0-8010-2012-3
    1. Psychology and religion. 2. Psychology—Religious aspects—Christianity. I. Title.
    BF51.F38   1995
    261.5′15—dc20   94-47067

An instructor's manual, including test items, is available for this book. Professors should contact the publisher.

Contents

9l557

Foreword

"Are we nothing but brain impulses?" "Should Christians use techniques of influence?" "What about hypnosis?" "ESP?" These are some of the questions that I met as I read my prepublication copy of Harold Faw's *Psychology in Christian Perspective: An Analysis of Key Issues.*

They are questions that Christian students—and others—frequently ask psychologists. Professor Faw knows. For many years he has taught courses in introductory psychology as well as senior seminars dealing with the integration of psychology and Christianity. I also know, because Christian students ask me similar questions. This is why I am so pleased to see the questions faced squarely in this concise volume.

Modern psychology was born little more than one hundred years ago in the laboratories of German physiologists. It was quickly adopted and nurtured through the first part of this century by American pragmatists. Gradually, it increased in popularity and influence until no part of society was left untouched. Now, at the end of the twentieth century, many parts of North American society are beginning to question their optimistic embrace of psychology. Religious communities that were often swept up with psychology's initial welcome are also beginning to reexamine their position. They are, like Christian psychologist Paul Vitz, "placing today's psychology in a much smaller, less corrosive, but ultimately more accurate and more helpful perspective" (1994, x).

Placing psychology in an accurate perspective is a challenge for every student of psychology. In fact it is a task for every concerned member of modern western culture. In twelve thoughtful chapters Professor Faw carefully brings important issues into view and helps his readers gain perspective. His respect for the scientific tools of psychology and for psychology's accumulated knowledge is balanced by a deep reverence and awe at the marvels of human thought and behavior.

I invite you—whether in a formal classroom setting or on your own—to let Professor Faw stimulate your critical thinking and place "psychology in Christian perspective."

Ronald P. Philipchalk

Vitz, P. C. 1994. *Psychology as religion: The cult of self-worship.* 2d ed. Grand Rapids: Eerdmans.

Preface

Psychology presents an incredible array of topics, ranging from neurotransmitters to memory failure to cultic conversion. Those of us working in this fascinating field are excited about both the challenges we face and the progress already made. At the same time, we must remember that psychology is a human creation; it contains a mix of truth and distortion.

I have one major purpose in writing *Psychology in Christian Perspective*: to stimulate you to think about the relationship between your Christian faith and contemporary psychology. This is an exciting and significant enterprise. After we have analyzed this relationship together, I hope you will agree.

As I prepared *Psychology in Christian Perspective*, I had a variety of readers in mind. Some of you will be students in an introductory psychology course. For you, these pages will supplement other sources of insight about psychology—your professor, other textbooks, classroom demonstrations. Some of you will read to enhance your personal understanding of what psychology is and how it fits with your beliefs about life, God, and yourself. I hope that each of you will experience a growing appreciation for and commitment to both God's Word and the field of psychology.

You will find the content of each chapter organized in a consistent fashion to help you to find your way. Each has four main elements. The first lays the groundwork for the chapter. It consists of an opening narrative, a short section highlighting a theme or a person, and a brief overview of the major topics included in standard introductory psychology texts. The second unit involves a more extended discussion of one specific issue in which there appears to be tension between psychology and faith. It presents a range of Christian views and then suggests one way to resolve the tension. The third component of each chapter explores one or two topics in which psychological and biblical perspectives are mutually beneficial, or psychological findings are especially useful to Christians. The final part recaps the chapter and suggests several additional readings that you may consult for deeper insight.

I gratefully acknowledge the varied contributions that many people have made to this project. My editor, Jim Weaver, was encouraging and accommodating throughout the process. Several colleagues read portions of the manuscript and offered valuable suggestions. Students in my seminar class stimulated my thinking and made helpful comments. Finally, my wife, Fern, and sons, Rick and Kevin, hung in there with me. They may be even more delighted than I that the book is finally done!

If in reading this book, you gain a little clearer perspective on psychology, my efforts will have been amply rewarded. Any comments on what you will read are most welcome. Please send your reactions and suggestions to me at Baker Book House.

1

Foundational
Issues and Perspectives

Imagine that you have just taken a seat in the classroom on day one of your first psychology course. Glancing around you with a mixture of concern and anticipation, you begin wondering what the course will be like. Will I find psychology tedious and trivial, or will it capture my imagination? What is psychology anyhow? Your inner dialogue is interrupted as the professor asks each student to take a piece of paper and complete the following sentence: "In my view, a psychologist is someone who . . ." What's this—a test already? It's only the first day, and we haven't been taught anything yet!

I regularly give this task to unsuspecting freshman students on opening day in psychology classes. It is one of several questions through which I attempt to better understand their thinking. Invariably, students provide an enlightening array of responses: In my view, a psychologist is someone who . . .

"helps individuals deal with life."
"knows a lot about the human mind and human behavior."
"cares, who listens, and who is willing to help people through difficulties."
"gets paid to listen to other people's problems."
"analyzes a person and what makes him tick."
"uses big words and analyzes everything and anything."

If you are new to psychology, your response might be similar to one of these.

The range in both the content and the tone of these opinions indicates the variation in perspective with which people approach the study of psychology. Some are particularly naive, while others are remarkably well informed. Some hold views that have obviously been shaped by the media, whereas others base their perspective on direct acquaintance with a psychologist. All demonstrate at least a rough idea of what psychology is.

Psychology can be described as a systematic attempt to understand human behavior and conscious experience. Unlike some other fields with similar goals, psychology seeks its insight primarily through observation and science rather than through reasoning or speculation. This distinctive offers a strong attraction; every September, thousands of eager students enroll in their first psychology course, hoping to learn more about this fascinating subject.

Psychology's Wide Appeal

For numbers of these students, their introductory course will be the first of many, for on college campuses across North America, psychology is among the most popular majors available. How can we account for the widespread popularity of this growing discipline? Several reasons come to mind.

Most of us are intensely curious about the mysteries of our own and others' behaviors, be they commonplace or bizarre. Probably every one of us has been frustrated by the experience of retaining trivial details from a recent movie, yet completely forgetting even the central point of yesterday afternoon's lecture. Who among us, having encountered a tragically aloof autistic child or a mentally handicapped but cheerful adult, is not both repulsed and attracted at the same time? And what normal person is not curious about how, within moments, we can identify the voice of a long-lost friend who phones unexpectedly? The challenge of a better understanding of ourselves beckons both researchers and students to embark upon the journey of exploring human experience. For this author, after more than twenty years of pondering, learning, and teaching, the love affair with psychology shows no sign of cooling off.

But there is more. Those of us fortunate enough to work or study at an institution committed to biblical perspectives on life and learning have an additional reason to study psychology. This motivation may be even more compelling than our natural curiosity. Upon completing the creation of the world and its colorful array of inhabitants, God adopted the role of evaluator and graded what he had made as *good* (Gen. 1). Having completed the task of creating humans, however, God evaluated his work as being *very good*. We have the opportunity of examining and marveling at his excellent work.

Due to the tragic effects of our first parents' fall into sin, people as we now find them are not functioning according to God's original design. Nevertheless, there remains an essential reflection of the Creator in all humankind, tarnished and distorted though it certainly is. Consequently, delving into the mysteries of human thought and behavior brings with it treasures of insight into our awesome Creator-God. Thus for the Christian, the investigation of human experience is motivated not only by a desire to understand ourselves, but also by a hunger to know God more fully.

Let us ponder for a moment along with David the marvelous way in which God has made us. In Psalm 139, David revels in the wonder of both God's creative power as seen in humans and his incredibly intimate knowledge of each person. These verses are worth meditating on thoughtfully and often, for they draw us along with the psalmist into wonder and worship. "You know when I sit and when I rise; you perceive my thoughts from afar. You discern my going out and my lying down; you are familiar with all my ways" (vv. 2–3). "For you created my inmost being; you knit me together in my mother's womb. I praise you because I am fearfully and wonderfully made; your works are wonderful, I know that full well" (vv. 13–14). For the child of God, the study of psychology engenders an attitude of humility and awe—we can praise our great God even as we pursue insight into people, his image-bearers.

Surveying the Landscape

Before we begin our explorations, let's pause briefly and scan the major contours of the region ahead. Psychology is an incredibly broad and varied discipline, incorporating a startling array of topics and perspectives. At one pole, it borders on the disciplines of biology and medicine, sometimes joining them in an attempt to alleviate the tragic consequences of brain disease or injury. At the other pole, psychology intersects the fields of sociology and anthropology in their explorations of how group norms and social context affect an individual's actions. A striking example of this unfortunate influence occurs when mobs engage in senseless acts of violence and vandalism.

Between these poles lie a myriad of aspects of human functioning. Psychologists investigate age-related shifts in children's reasoning abilities, bizarre behavior changes brought about by mental illness, variations of human personality traits, and much more. Psychology has numerous subfields. Specialists in the dynamics of small-group interaction will conduct studies that share little in common with the research of those exploring the perception and recognition of human faces.

In addition to these obvious differences in topic or specialty, psychologists adopt a wide range of underlying perspectives in their efforts to understand the mysteries of our humanness. Some researchers are committed to a *neurobiological* approach, searching for causes of abnormalities such as schizophrenia in the patterns of brain-cell activity. Others, commonly known as *behaviorists*, look for links between the events in an individual's physical or social environment and his or her outward actions. Those preferring a *cognitive* approach find the parallel between human and computer processing of information both intriguing and instructive. A psychologist who opts for the *humanistic* approach rejects the restrictive and dehumanizing scientific rigor of these experimentally oriented methods, emphasizing instead the unique human qualities of choice, feeling, and self-determination. Finally, those who, like Freud, believe in the powerful role of the unconscious, approach their investigations from a *psychoanalytic* perspective. Researchers who prefer very different approaches may at times focus on the same human experience but investigate it at quite different levels. We will have more to say on this important point shortly.

Given the rich complexity and endless variety of human experience, it should not surprise you that the tools used to explore those experiences also range rather widely. It is worth noting, however, that all these strategies are based in some way on direct observation and are thus part of the general method known as science. Let's briefly introduce the most common techniques.

Some investigators choose to conduct experiments, a method in which cause-and-effect patterns are explored. This is done by controlling situational variables as much as possible, manipulating potential causes of behavior, and noting the changes that follow. For many researchers, particularly those enamored by the precision and the objectivity of science, this method is the most preferred.

Other procedures are much less intrusive. In many observational studies—for example, those exploring play patterns in children—participants are unaware that their behavior is being recorded. Other descriptive methods, some perhaps already familiar to you, include surveys, questionnaires, interviews, and correlational studies. The latter are designed to discover whether variables such as friendliness and intelligence are related. No particular attempt is made to determine specific causal links.

Armed with this preliminary understanding of the scope of psychology and the range of research strategies it employs, we turn to a fundamental issue. It is one we address now and come back to again and again throughout the book.

Are Psychology and Faith Compatible?

The basic question that challenges every thoughtful Christian who looks seriously at psychology can be phrased in various ways. Christian psychologist Gary Collins (1988) expressed it simply in the title of his recent book *Can You Trust Psychology?* Alternatively, we might ask, Can psychology be compatible with genuine Christian faith? This is a question to which sincere believers have given a variety of answers.

According to James Beck and James Banks (1992), there are three distinct views about the place that psychology should occupy in the life and thought of the evangelical Christian community. One group of Christians welcomes psychology, incorporating its concepts freely into both understanding and practice and attempting to equate theological and psychological concepts whenever possible. Robert Schuller's strong emphasis on self-esteem and positive thinking illustrates this first view (Schuller 1982).

A second group of believers is wary of psychology and often strongly critical of it. These believers regard it as a threat to the purity of true Christian faith and as a movement that directly competes with an orthodox biblical position. The forceful anti-psychology writings of David Hunt (1987) and Martin and Deidre Bobgan (1987) represent this second viewpoint.

A third group of Christians holds a more central position. For them, psychology is a source of useful insight, but one that, because of the influence of anti-Christian perspectives, must be carefully evaluated in light of biblical teaching. Attempts to combine biblical and psychological understanding of human nature and experience, including the present work, grow out of this third position.

Many thoughtful people are troubled and confused by the array of conflicting positions held by orthodox believers, all of whom claim a genuine commitment to Christ. In the minds of some, there must be one correct position on this issue; we need to discover it and then persuade all Christians to adopt it. A few claim to have already found the correct and final answer.

All too frequently, in our commendable search for truth, we reject any perspective that differs from our own without understanding it or seriously considering its merit. Sometimes we resort to discrediting the integrity of those who hold opposing views in order to resolve inner confusion and bolster our confidence. Although I have a defensible position on the issue of how psychology and Christian faith relate, I do not believe that everyone should necessarily adopt my particular view.

Naturally, I hope that my readers will carefully consider the perspectives presented in this book. However, understanding our differing views and the basis for each is to me much more important than convincing others to accept the "correct position." In case you don't agree with this claim, consider the following defense for an approach based on tolerance and understanding.

As confirmed by both Scripture and psychology, all of us see "through a glass darkly" (1 Cor. 13:12 KJV). It is important for Christians to understand and affirm that objective and absolute truth exists and is known with complete accuracy by God. We must also understand, however, that no one except God enjoys this luxury. In contrast to his understanding, ours is always colored by errors and distortions that result from human fallibility. Several factors might cause different people to arrive at diverse conclusions as to how psychology and Christianity relate. Let us consider some of these.

Sources of Disparity

Evangelical Christians share a common commitment to the Word of God as inspired and authoritative. Consequently, they all have much the same understanding of such fundamental doctrines as the character of God, the deity of Christ, the seriousness of sin, and the means of man's reconciliation with God. On less central issues, however, we interpret the same Scriptures in a variety of ways (Johnson 1983). Often these differences arise from diversities in our cultural and theological roots.

Some hold a separatist view, placing top priority on preservation of the purity of our faith and prevention of contamination from unchristian influences. Others emphasize our responsibility to function as salt and light in society, interacting with and challenging our culture with Christian perspectives and values. These differences (often functioning at an unconscious level) predispose us to expect either serious discrepancies or fundamental harmony. As is frequently our experience, we tend to find what we are looking for.

Our unique life histories and personalities can also influence our reading of Scripture. Some people are by nature inclined to know the correct position and to be annoyed that others can't see it. Others are more willing to tolerate uncertainty. Depending on our unique experiences and our direct contacts with psychologists, we may form a negative or a positive impression that colors all subsequent evaluation.

These considerations help us to understand why various believers interpret Scripture quite differently. Cedric Johnson (1983) emphasizes the impact such influences can have by arguing that there is no such thing as a biblical fact that bypasses human interpretation. Although God's Word is absolute and infallible, our understanding of it clearly is not. Open discussion of ideas and thoughtful evaluation of differing viewpoints in the context of mutual trust and humble truth-seeking are vital. They help to counteract our ever-present human tendency to err.

One other factor merits consideration in this context. As we have already seen, psychology comprises a wide range of specialty areas. The probability of tension and conflict arising between psychology and Christian belief is much greater in areas such as counseling or personality theory than in specialties such as visual perception or causes of forgetting. So depending on which specialty area is the focus of one's evaluation, the degree to which psychology and an orthodox Christian position can be compatible varies widely. A single summary assessment cannot do justice to the entire field. This point will become clearer as we examine a variety of controversial topics in subsequent chapters.

Two Key Questions

Without making any claim of having identified the only Christian position on this or any other issue to be discussed in the book, I will shortly make clear my own starting assumptions. Readers are invited to evaluate these perspectives for themselves. Before doing so, however, let's consider two important preliminary questions. They involve the appropriateness of seeking knowledge from sources outside the Bible and the ability of unbelievers to discover and report truth (Jones 1986, 29–31).

The Bible's own claims to sufficiency (for example, 2 Tim. 3:16–17) are sometimes interpreted to mean that reliance on wisdom from extrabiblical sources is forbidden. Yet few if any Christians live consistently with this interpretation. All of us use the products of science and technology, take advantage of the discoveries of medical research, consult lawyers and accountants for advice, and watch news broadcasts on television. Do these activities run counter to the thrust of scriptural teaching? Not really. Rather than avoiding the use of extrabiblical sources of insights, we need to evaluate the information they provide within the framework of a Christian understanding of truth and life.

For the believer, humanly derived knowledge based on God's general revelation (his creation) never extends beyond the framework that special revelation (the Bible) provides. However, by using the tools of observation that God has permitted us to develop and apply, we can fill in important and useful information on topics that the Bible does not address in detail. This is a worthwhile activity, compatible with our God-ordained role as stewards of his universe. However, our investigation of God's creation must never replace or compete with the foundation for understanding provided through God's Word, the Bible. For the Christian, truth from any source must either be consistent with this framework or be judged less than truth.

Turning to the second preliminary issue, let us ponder briefly the matter of whether unbelievers can discover truth. It is useful to distinguish between truth about reconciliation with our Creator, a topic on which he alone has the authority to speak, and truth about various aspects of ordinary human experience. God's Word is the sole source of the information we need to be rightly related to him. Human wisdom has nothing to add, and claims of alternative paths to God must be rejected. But in the realm of our present experience, the Bible leaves a great deal unsaid. For example, it does not address in any direct way the question of whether children experiencing severe abuse should be removed from their natural families. Instead, it provides the large framework of respect and love for all persons within which this and many other specific issues need to be considered.

The view held by trusted Christian thinkers over the centuries is that legitimate insight can arise from human sources, both Christian and non-Christian. As an expression of his grace, the God who created humankind with curiosity, reasoning ability, and creative talent permits people to find truth. Their grasp of this truth is always incomplete and frequently distorted due to human sinfulness and fallibility. Indeed, even believers have only a partial grasp of truth, for all of us inhabit a fallen world in which the effects of sin persist. Thus, all human insight needs to be checked against the parameters laid out in Scripture. We will differ somewhat on exactly what these parameters are, but we agree that they exist and must be taken into account. They provide the guidance needed to prevent us from all too easily becoming victims of our own foolish imaginations.

A Personal Starting Point

In considering any issue, Christians need to think both care-fully and biblically rather than to accept what someone pro-claims as truth. Each person approaches a topic with a variety of prior beliefs, and these assumptions shape the individual's conclusions. Let me now make explicit some of my basic assumptions, not as a prescription for others to follow, but as a means of clarifying my point of view.

I approach psychology and questions about its relationship to Christian belief from the following fundamental point of view:

1. God alone is self-sufficient, dependent on no one else for his existence. By contrast, I am a contingent being, fully dependent on him for every breath, and ultimately accountable to him. As succinctly expressed by James Sire, "God is God and I am not" (1990, 15).
2. God is the source and author of all truth, whether it is discovered through study of his special revelation, the Bible, or his general revelation, the universe and all within it. He perfectly and completely understands this truth; in contrast, my grasp of it is incomplete and error-prone.
3. Due to differing interpretations of either Scripture, psychological data, or both, numerous discrepancies in our understanding can arise. However, these differences ought not to interfere with our ability to enjoy fellowship with those with whom we may happen to disagree.
4. I have a great deal to learn from both believers and un-believers. Honest dialogue—both listening in order to truly understand and clearly articulating our own views—is essential to progress in our corporate search for truth.

So far, we have examined the nature and breadth of the field of psychology and have explored the fundamental issue of its relationship with Christian faith. We conclude this chapter by considering how psychological and Christian perspectives can each contribute to the other in a constructive way.

A Mutually Beneficial Interchange

We have discussed five of the common perspectives with which different psychologists approach their study of human experience. Further reflection shows that each one of these viewpoints is both correct and incorrect at the same time. Let's try to see how this is so.

In the *neurobiological* approach, people are regarded as extremely complex physical machines. At one level, this is accurate, and we will see examples of the wonder of our neurological complexity, particularly in chapters 2 and 3. But humans are also much more than this. We are creative and reflective persons who are capable of making real choices, rather than helpless products of our neurons' firing patterns. So while this approach provides a valuable perspective, it is far too limited to include the whole picture.

The *behavioral* approach highlights the important role played by the social environment in influencing human activities and the power that rewards and punishments have over us. We will be able to relate to and understand others much better if we take these factors into account. But to stop here misses a whole dimension of human nature in which we take the initiative in changing our environment and choosing courses of action that no one could have predicted. This viewpoint is valuable, although too limited.

To some extent, the *cognitive* approach makes room for our ability to choose, but points toward some of the bases for these choices. We are free to choose, but our selections are not random ones. They are based on information that we have taken in, sorted, stored, and subsequently retrieved and that we judge to be relevant to the current situation. So information is critical in much of what we do. But our behaviors are not based exclusively on mental activities. We must not ignore the influence of habits, emotions, and hormones as well. So while this approach provides helpful insight, it too is incomplete.

Does the *humanistic* approach fare any better? Its emphasis on uniquely human characteristics of choice, feeling, and self-determination are a welcome relief from the confining and mechanistic perspectives that dominate most of the other viewpoints. This approach has been particularly popular in North America.

Partly as a result of progress in health care, education, and scientific pursuits, our society affords opportunities to develop our unique potential to a greater extent than has been possible at most times and places in history. For that we can be grateful. What is woefully inadequate about this view, however, is its refusal to recognize our human limitations and our strong bent toward evil. It gives no adequate answer to the nagging question of why the world contains so much injustice, grief, and tragedy.

The *psychoanalytic* view is in many ways the polar opposite of the popular humanistic approach. It emphasizes a side of human nature that represents our inherent evil, whereby our choices are powerfully slanted in selfish and destructive directions. But if, as this viewpoint suggests, we are the victims of inner forces and impulses, how can we legitimately be held accountable for our poor choices?

When we reflect on these varied viewpoints, the resulting picture is quite like the one that emerged when several blind men examined and then attempted to describe an elephant. Depending on what part of the animal each man made contact with, he found this puzzling creature similar to a rope, a tree trunk, or a wall. Each description was accurate but too limited. In much the same way, each of these five approaches to psychology offers a helpful perspective on the totality of human experience. However, each is also seriously distorted if it is assumed to provide a complete account. It is true that by combining all five perspectives, or adopting what is often called a *holistic* approach, we will achieve an understanding that is closer to reality. However, there is value in going a step further and placing all of these views within a biblical framework.

Biblical Perspectives on Humanness

The concept of persons presented in the Bible is one of contrasts. The apostle Paul declares that "all have sinned and fall short of the glory of God" (Rom. 3:23). The psalmist concurs with this distressing characterization: "All have turned aside; they have together become corrupt; there is no one who does good, not even one" (Ps. 14:3). Yet, the creation account affirms, "So God created man in his own image" (Gen. 1:27), and David marvels concerning man, "You made him a little lower than the heavenly beings and crowned him with glory and honor" (Ps. 8:5). Since both perspectives are unmistakably and repeatedly affirmed in Scripture, we do well to begin by affirming the dual nature of man.

Regarding humans as a puzzling union of both exalted and fallen natures has been common among orthodox Christians. However, the relative emphasis placed on each side of this nature has varied enormously. Some have concluded that the consequences of the fall as described in Genesis 3 are so pervasive that all God-like characteristics with which we left the hand of the Creator have been obliterated. In the understanding of others, our fallenness has drastic eternal consequences, but limited implications in the present life.

Frequently, such discussions revolve around the question of what the image of God in man entails. Arthur Holmes (1983) argues that our *relatedness* and our *responsibility* are the primary aspects of the image of God that all humans reflect. Mary Van Leeuwen (1985) identifies *accountable dominion* as the most distinctive mark of this concept. Frequently, characteristic human capacities such as reasoning ability, moral sensitivity, creative potential, language facility, and God-consciousness are considered to be further aspects of the divine image. But perhaps more important than spelling out the probable components of this concept is the fact that we understand the entire notion in its proper context.

Psalm 8 provides the most detailed case for *The Majesty of Man* (Allen 1984). In it, the entire picture of the apex of God's creative genius is framed within the opening and closing verses of the psalm: "O LORD, our Lord, how majestic is your name in all the earth." This truth is well worth pondering. The antidote to secular humanism with its inflated, self-centered concept of the person is not to deny the majesty of man, but to see it in its proper context. That context is clearly the majesty of God our Creator who chose to make man the pinnacle of his work. We do indeed have dignity and worth, not because of what we have accomplished, but because of who God is and because of his choice to make us in his own incomparable image.

It is essential that our efforts to understand people begin with the framework provided by a biblical perspective on life, knowledge, and humanness. Within these parameters, each of the common approaches in the field of psychology has a useful contribution to make. One way to reconcile these apparently incompatible perspectives is to think in terms of different *levels of explanation* or viewing distances. Some approaches represent an effort to examine small details at close range (neurobiological), while others involve standing further back in order to see the larger picture (humanistic). Myers and Jeeves (1987, 6) offer a helpful analogy: "It's like viewing a masterpiece painting. If you stand right up against it, you will understand better how the paint was applied, but you will miss completely the subject and impact of the painting as a whole." Although they may appear to be incompatible, each approach offers a different and useful perspective on a single complex reality—humankind, the apex of God's creation.

Reflecting Back

In this chapter, the recurring theme has been **diversity**. The field of psychology comprises many specialties. Each appears to have little in common with the others, but all are united in their attempt to unravel some aspect of the mystery of human experience. The methods of investigation employed are also varied, but share in common the choice of observing people directly rather than attempting to use reasoning and logical deduction alone. Likewise, the range of perspectives that are adopted reflect focus on different aspects of the complexity of human nature or different viewing distances.

Exploring the fundamental issue of whether psychology can be compatible with a conservative Christian view, we discovered that different Christians have arrived at different conclusions. We noted that several cultural and personal factors contribute to these differences in perspective, despite a common commitment to the authority of Scripture. We then examined one topic (approaches to psychology) to discover how insights from psychological research and Christian theology can be mutually enriching, provided we operate within the framework of a biblical view of humanness. In succeeding chapters, we will explore examples of both points of tension and opportunities for beneficial dialogue between Christian belief and the discipline of psychology.

Going Deeper

1. For balanced comments on a variety of interesting questions about psychology and Christian belief, see Gary Collins's *Can You Trust Psychology?* (InterVarsity, 1988).
2. For an excellent treatment of the nature of man in the tradition of Christian humanism, consult Ronald Allen's *The Majesty of Man* (Multnomah, 1984).
3. For help in learning to think clearly and critically about your position on tough issues, I recommend Mark McMinn's and James Foster's *Christians in the Crossfire* (Barclay, 1990).
4. For insight into the development and possible future direction of Christian opposition to psychology, consult "Christian anti-psychology sentiment: Hints of an historical analogue" by James Beck and James Banks, *Journal of Psychology and Theology* 20 (1992): 3–10.
5. For an illuminating treatment of various positions Christians take on the integration of psychology and Christianity, see chapter 1 of Stan Jones's *Psychology and the Christian Faith* (Baker, 1986).

2

Brain and Behavior

It began like a thousand other early autumn days in Vermont, but before it was over, the life of Phineas Gage was changed forever. A railroad construction foreman, he was preparing to blast away a large section of rock. A hole had been drilled in the rock, and Gage was using a steel rod to pack gunpowder into the hole. When the powder exploded unexpectedly, his tamping rod, thicker than a broom handle and nearly as long, became a missile. It was driven into the side of his face and out the top of his head, landing on the ground some distance away.

To the amazement of his co-workers, Gage did not die instantly. In fact, he was conscious during the cart ride into town, climbed a long flight of stairs, and carried on a conversation with the local doctor who attended to his injury. Despite massive loss of blood and serious infection from the wound, Gage made a remarkable recovery, and within about two months was walking around the town, looking almost normal. But to those who knew Gage, it was painfully obvious that his personality had been radically altered. Formerly a calm, reliable, and mild-mannered person, he became unpredictable and abusive, often displaying a violent temper. He had trouble maintaining his focus on the task at hand, and despite his physical health, lost his job with the railroad. After traveling around the continent as a fairground curiosity, he died twelve years later.

Brain and Mind: A Puzzling Union

For centuries, philosophers have pondered the relationship between our minds and our bodies. Is one real and the other imaginary, or are both equally real? Do they consist of the same stuff, or are two different substances involved? The contemporary version of this ancient question asks how the brain and mind are related. The tragic experiences of Phineas Gage and other victims of brain injury give this theoretical debate a note of practical relevance and urgency.

In attempting to come to terms with the question of brain-mind connections, most current thinkers adopt one of three main positions: dualism, monism, or perspectivalism. Let's decode these terms and catch at least a glimpse of the underlying issues.

Dualism asserts that the mind and the brain (or the body) are two separate and distinct substances, one material and the other nonmaterial. This position has history on its side, being supported by many of the ancient Greek philosophers, as well as by more recent thinkers such as René Descartes and by contemporary brain researchers such as Wilder Penfield. The intuitive appeal of this view resides in the fact that we all know that our bodies have a tangible, physical quality that our thoughts, feelings, and wishes obviously lack. For Christians, this view is comfortable and widely accepted because it effectively preserves the legitimacy of both material and nonmaterial worlds. However, the close links repeatedly observed between our physical bodies and our mental and emotional experiences are hard to account for within a dualistic framework.

With some notable exceptions, contemporary secular thinkers and scientists have adopted a position called *monism*. From this perspective, there is only one kind of reality—the material world we know through our senses. All else is reducible to the physical; there is no separate nonphysical realm. Monists do not deny the existence of mind or thought. They argue that it can be readily explained in terms of its physical basis (the brain) without reference to a separate kind of substance. With this view, Christians are generally uneasy, for it provides no place for the soul or the spirit of mankind.

A number of contemporary Christian thinkers discern in Scripture an unmistakable emphasis on the wholeness and unity of human nature. They adopt a *perspectivalist* view, suggesting that we are a mind-body unity—a single reality that can be examined from many different perspectives or levels. This position preserves the notion of unity, but it leaves unanswered the puzzling question of what happens to us at death, when the body ceases to function. Does the person also cease to exist until the resurrection?

The mind-body problem represents a puzzling challenge to explore, one that is not easily resolved. Debate will no doubt continue and perhaps intensify as researchers contribute new insight into how the brain functions as it influences and is influenced by the emotional, spiritual, and mental dimensions of the individual.

The Brain: Hub of All Our Experience

The keen interest that psychologists have shown in the human body is focused largely on the brain. This is not surprising, for our brains exert a powerful influence on our behavior and mental life. The basic building blocks of our brain and nervous system are the *neurons* or individual nerve cells. Each neuron consists of three basic parts: the branchlike *dendrites* through which messages from neighboring cells are received, the core of the cell, called the *cell body*, and the longer, stretched-out *axon* through which impulses are sent on. A single human brain is thought to contain many billions of neurons.

Our neurons are in constant communication with one another. Impulses travel along the axon of a given cell, eventually reaching the end. There they must cross a gap or *synapse* between this cell and its neighbor. The transmission of impulses both within and between neurons has been the subject of careful study, for in some sense, all human experience is dependent on the activities of these cells. In particular, the chemistry of synaptic transmission, probably the key to understanding how drugs influence behavior, has been the focus of a good deal of recent attention. The processes that unfold at the synapses are complex and awe-inspiring. Throughout our bodies, they occur countless times per second with amazing reliability.

Knowledge of the precise role played by specific regions of the brain is still limited, for researchers face a huge challenge when they attempt to unlock the brain's secrets. Besides dissecting and examining the brains of animals, scientists use various techniques such as monitoring brain wave patterns, plotting the distribution of blood flow throughout the brain, and listening in on the conversation of the neurons by means of tiny electronic microphones. In addition, a great deal has been learned from the behavioral consequences of brain injury caused by accidents, tumors, or brain surgery.

The lower centers of your brain are perched on top of the spinal cord near the middle of your head. They serve similar life-maintaining functions for us as they do for other mammals, controlling breathing, blood flow, digestion, and so on. Their protected location is significant, for without these essential functions, you could not survive for even a minute.

Greater differences between animal and human brains are found in the upper and outer parts of the brain called the *cerebral cortex*. Although your cat's brain contains sensory areas for interpreting visual and auditory inputs, it lacks the large regions in the cortex that are linked to uniquely human capacities such as planning for the future, being self-conscious in the present, and remembering a personal past. One particularly fascinating feature of the human brain is the fact that it comprises two distinct halves or *hemispheres* that are similar in appearance but have quite different functions. For most people, the left half seems to specialize in logical or sequential processing of information. By contrast, the right half is believed to deal holistically and intuitively with the information it receives.

Without the entire nervous system, the brain would be unable to serve our needs, for it must communicate with the rest of the body. Chains of neurons in the *somatic nervous system* receive data from our sense organs, including skin and muscles, and convey the brain's motor commands to our muscles. A second equally complex network called the *autonomic nervous system* monitors and controls the activities of inner organs. This system operates without our awareness, making it possible to digest our food and read psychology books at the same time.

From this whirlwind tour of the human brain and nervous system, we turn to the perplexing and controversial question of brain control. We will discover that knowledge of brain functioning has potential for both use and misuse.

Brain Control: Solution or Problem?

Brain functioning powerfully affects behavior, a fact that is clear from cases of head injuries, tumors, strokes, and diseases of the brain. When surgery is performed or drugs are prescribed to halt tissue damage or to correct clear imbalances in the brain's chemistry, no one objects. This kind of intervention seems appropriate, even though it may carry with it a risk of undesired side effects. But what about intervening deliberately by surgical, electrical, or chemical means when the causes of the person's problems may not be located in the physical brain? Consider the following examples.

During the 1940s and 1950s, thousands of psychiatric patients in North America and elsewhere underwent a surgical procedure known as a *frontal leucotomy*. In this particular surgery, large bundles of nerve fiber connecting the frontal lobes (located just behind the forehead) with other regions of the brain were cut. Basing the procedure in part on the results of experimental studies with animals, surgeons reasoned that patients showing agitation and extreme distress were suitable candidates for a frontal leucotomy. Although many of the patients treated in this way did become more subdued, they frequently showed loss of initiative, creativity, and purpose.

A dramatic demonstration of brain control in animals (and potentially in people as well) is found in Jose Delgado's unusual bullfighting methods. Pictures of Delgado facing a charging bull in the ring sometimes appear in psychology books. He is armed not with the traditional bullfighter's cape, but with a radio transmitter. A number of tiny electrodes are implanted in specific targets in the limbic system of the bull's brain. When Delgado activates these from a distance, the bull's deadly charge is halted. The animal becomes confused and seems to forget its aggressive intent. Could the same effect be achieved in humans who are particularly prone to violent actions?

Probably more familiar to many of us are children who have trouble paying attention and who display restlessness and almost constant movement. The exact cause of their hyperactivity is not known, but it is common to treat the behavior by chemical means. As a result, these children typically become easier to manage and often get along better with their peers as well. However, neither the immediate side effects nor the long-term results of this type of treatment are well understood.

As a final example, suppose that a friend or a relative battles continually with severe depression and speaks often about ending his life. Although no physical root for the depression has been identified, efforts to deal with it through counseling and prescription drugs have been ineffective. Would you be willing to permit one or more electroconvulsive therapy (ECT) treatments? Evidence suggests that most patients report feeling less depressed immediately after ECT, but a degree of memory loss is typical also. Longer-term impact is difficult to predict.

Put yourself in the place of a family member or a friend who is called upon to help choose a suitable course of action in any of the preceding cases. Would you support use of physical interventions? To what extent should the patient be permitted to choose or to refuse such treatment? Relatives and friends will be affected by these decisions. How much input should they have? What about the side effects of these procedures? Would you urge an initially reluctant individual to accept treatment? What guiding criteria would you use in making these difficult choices?

These examples remind us that problem behaviors can often be altered through direct intervention in the brain. Even though the specific procedures—surgical, electrical, or chemical—are diverse, the underlying question remains the same: Is it appropriate to seek physical solutions to problems that appear to be primarily personal or social in their origin? Is brain control a solution or could it be a problem?

The Perspective of Faith

The basis for a balanced perspective on this issue is found in a proper understanding of personhood. Every individual has immense value in the eyes of God, having been created in his magnificent image. We are inclined to judge people in terms of their functional value—what they can contribute to the lives of others and to their society. If deeply depressed or brain-injured persons are unable to function in society, they are automatically seen as less valuable. We need to keep in mind that human worth as God values it is much more intrinsic—we each have dignity and worth because he made us to reflect his person and nature, regardless of how our contribution to society compares with that of other people.

A related perspective has to do with the place of technology in dealing with human problems. It is all too easy to brush aside concepts of accountability to God and each other and to opt for the quickest and easiest solutions we can find. We need to pause and reflect carefully before resorting to brain intervention when a person's behavior does not conform with society's norms or our expectations. We may be in danger of opting for quick and convenient solutions to complex problems that call for our commitment, care, and compassion. Our accountability before God for our relations with one another needs to be kept in the forefront of all considerations of brain control.

Why are some Christians more willing than others to implement physical interventions through chemicals or brain surgery? I suspect that most of us would consider surgical or chemical treatments if we were desperate and were convinced that counseling and loving support no longer held any hope of providing relief in a crisis. But wide disparity would be evident as different people decided whether such a point had been reached. In addition, our views of how the brain and the person are related could make a practical difference. If the person and the brain are regarded as an inseparable and harmonious unity, we might be less inclined to permit direct intervention in the brain. A dualistic perspective offers some justification for tampering with the brain, however, for from that viewpoint, it is distinct and separate from the mind or soul—the essence of the person.

Sifting Through the Options

It should be evident that the issues with which we have been grappling are extremely complex. No easy solutions are available. Cases in which brain control might be considered will be highly individual and unique, calling for informed, prayerful, and compassionate courses of action from those who are involved. Persistent behavior problems such as severe depression, extreme behavior disturbances, or strong tendencies toward violent and destructive activity cry out for practical solutions. As a context for the challenging task of choosing among available options, several considerations are worth emphasizing.

Evidence regarding the probable causes of the problem must first be carefully weighed. In cases involving hormone imbalance, destruction of brain tissue, or abnormal neurological patterns, physical treatments are appropriate. The issue is whether we have sufficient knowledge to implement an effective treatment. But behavioral difficulties can have roots in emotional or spiritual realms as well as physical ones. Their causes are often complex, perhaps involving a combination of factors from various domains—personal history, physical functioning, emotional trauma, and so on. In these cases where causes are not readily specified, physical interventions alone are highly suspect.

In cases in which a definite physical cause seems likely, the caliber of the appropriate brain treatment needs to be evaluated. An experimental procedure with uncertain benefits and with side effects about which we know little is unappealing. Human individuals are too precious to be regarded as little more than surgical guinea pigs.

Finally, the quality of the person's life and experience must be fundamental to our decisions. As Gareth Jones (1981) argues consistently, when someone's behavior and responses are impaired due to damage to the brain, the personhood that remains needs to be guarded and enhanced rather than jeopardized. Thus we need to weigh compassionately the likely impact that brain surgery or other interventions will have on the choices open to the individual. Those procedures that will add to their options are to be much preferred over those that further limit or restrict them.

Having considered some of the dangers of unwise use of our knowledge of the brain's functions, we now turn to focus on the wonder of its normal functioning. Many of the brain's miracles are reenacted every moment of our lives.

Fearfully and Wonderfully Made

In Psalm 139, David marvels at the Creator's design evident in the physical structure and development of the human body. We may assume that he understood little or nothing of how the brain and the nervous system function. Nevertheless, his attitude of wonder becomes more and more appropriate as brain researchers push back the frontiers of knowledge.

Resting unpretentiously under the protection of the bones of your skull, your brain—a three-pound lump of wet tissue, quite unimpressive in its appearance—is one of the most complex structures in existence. Although estimates vary considerably, the total number of neurons in your brain is probably several times greater than the entire human population. Because each neuron is connected with one thousand or more of its neighbors, and each link can be of significance, the brain's capacity to deal with information may be limitless.

To construct a mental picture of the complexity represented in a single human brain, Donald Mackay (1980, 23) uses a lecture-hall analogy. The neurons in the outer surface of the cortex provide most of the brain's vast information-processing capacity. This shell consists of a layer of greyish-colored cells approximately three millimeters thick. Due to the deep folds and wrinkles in this surface, its total area is a surprising two thousand square centimeters—roughly two and a half square feet. Now let's visualize one cubic millimeter of cortex (about the size of the tip of a sharp pencil) expanded to the size of a large classroom. It contains roughly one hundred thousand neurons, each with connecting links to thousands of its neighbors. The number of possible interconnections, each of potential significance in the job that the brain performs, would reach into the billions! And we are considering only one of the six hundred thousand cubic millimeters of tissue. On this same scale, our imaginary classrooms representing the whole flattened-out cortex would cover about twenty square miles when stacked three deep. Now that's a challenge for even the most skillful researcher!

Occurring with incredible speed and reliability, the moment-by-moment communication between neurons is a beautiful and delicate process. The chemical interchange that occurs at the gap between neurons, the *synapse,* is essential for even the most basic brain activity. When a particular cell fires, it sends an electrical impulse down the length of its axon, whose tip almost touches the dendrite tips of many of its neighbors. Then, a fascinating chemical process takes place in a flash—less than one thousandth of a second. The sending cell releases a chemical messenger called a *neurotransmitter* into the area between the cells. The molecules of this chemical that find their way to a receptor site in the receiving cell will attempt to persuade the second cell to respond appropriately. But simultaneously, hundreds of other neurons, all linked to the same receiving cell, are also exerting their influence in similar ways. As Michael Gazzaniga describes the process, "the neuron, like any good congressman, is listening to all its constituents before casting its vote to fire" (1988, 7).

More than two dozen different neurotransmitters have already been identified, each with its own unique chemical structure. Each needs to be supplied in exactly the correct amount for the brain to function effectively. It is not hard to see how even tiny doses of drugs that alter the production and the effect of these neurotransmitters can upset the delicate balance in the brain and can radically alter behavior.

Although the individual neurons in our brains operate much like those found in the brains of many animals, the human brain is different from any other in its overall structure. The presence of large frontal lobes, taking up nearly one third of the entire human brain, is unique. The fascinating differences between the left and the right hemispheres have received generous attention from both researchers and the public. For about 95 percent of us, the left hemisphere contains specific language sites and prefers to function in a logical and analytical fashion. The style of the right hemisphere is less clear, but it often operates in terms of global or intuitive judgments, as when we recognize a face in a single glance.

So far as we know, hemispheric differences comparable to those found in normal human brains do not occur in any nonhuman species. Despite this specialization of function, however, the two hemispheres work in harmony because they communicate constantly via the interconnecting bundle of nerve fibers called the *corpus callosum*. Working together, they equip us admirably for the range of cognitive tasks that we regularly encounter.

Damaged Goods

For centuries, the tragic consequences of brain damage have been a fact of life for many unfortunate individuals and their families. These cases serve as a sobering reminder that the human brain is the executive control center for the whole person. Without its efficient management of the enterprise, chaos reigns.

Reasons for breakdown in the brain's normally smooth operations are numerous. You have probably observed an older person who is partially or even totally paralyzed on one side due to a stroke. A stroke blocks the supply of blood to one or the other cerebral hemisphere, resulting in the immediate death of millions of neurons. Daily activities like walking, getting dressed, and speaking are then severely impaired.

Physical blows to the head such as those occurring in physical combat or traffic accidents may lead to relatively minor concussions or to much more serious and extensive impairment. Dreaded diseases such as Alzheimer's lead to a progressive loss of memory and personality structure, so that eventually the afflicted person is barely recognizable. Particularly vulnerable to abuse are the developing brains of prenatal infants. This is evident in the chronic emotional and behavioral difficulties faced by fetal alcohol children—infants whose mothers continued drinking extensively during pregnancy.

The behavioral consequences of injury to the brain are always negative ones and run along a few familiar lines. Varying degrees of memory loss, either from the very recent or the more distant past, are common. Disruption of motor coordination, making skilled and fluid movement difficult, are also typical. Depending on the area of the brain involved, loss of language capacity in the form of difficulty with speaking, reading, or understanding may occur. Recognition of formerly familiar objects or people may also become impossible. In some cases, even personality is changed, so that the individual's usual pattern of responding and relating with others is altered, often in impolite or embarrassing ways. Some brain damage causes emotional or mental problems, at times so severe that the person loses touch with the physical and social world in which he lives.

All of these changes represent behavior that is not typical of the person's former self, foreign to both the individual's history and the norms of society. The reaction of observers is often a mixture of curiosity and revulsion as, uncertain about how to respond, they withdraw from the changed person. Frequently, the focus of attention is on the losses in the individual's capacities and on the resulting behavioral limitations. But even a severely brain-damaged individual remains a person, although he or she cannot function in a normal human way. Options may be restricted, but so long as options and choices remain, the person should be permitted and encouraged to exercise them as fully as possible. Our interventions need to be motivated by compassion and directed toward expanding rather than further limiting the humanness that the injured person struggles to retain.

Throughout the New Testament accounts of the life of Jesus, we see him interacting almost constantly with those who for physical, emotional, or spiritual reasons were limited in certain ways. It is frequently said of Jesus that he was "moved with compassion" when he faced human need of any kind. His ministry was directed at restoring wholeness and full humanity together with reconciliation with God wherever these were lacking. Our response to those who have suffered brain damage needs to have the same objective and to be similarly motivated by compassion.

In cases of extreme damage to the brain, what remains of the persons are little more than shadows of what they once were. As Gareth Jones suggests, in some tragic cases, the body lives on despite the nearly complete death of the personality. In certain diseases associated with aging, the physical dimension of the person may far outlast mental or relational ones. Although any of us who experience such a condition, whether suddenly through brain injury or slowly through aging, will have restrictions on the expression of our personhood, we will not lose it entirely. Jones expresses it well: "If my brain is damaged, I may be less responsible, I may have many fewer courses of response open to me; I may be tragically limited; I may not even be aware of my limitations. Nevertheless, I am still a person" (1981, 112).

Reflecting Back

Throughout our consideration of the brain and its relation to human personality and behavior, the key word is **complexity**. A structure of amazing intricacy, the brain is sometimes referred to as the *last frontier* of human exploration. The structure of an individual neuron, the exquisite beauty of communication between one neuron and its neighbors, the marvelous balance and reliability of the everyday functioning of the entire human brain—all these direct our gaze to the God who designed this amazing structure.

Mushrooming knowledge of how the brain functions brings with it the lengthening shadow of a technology of brain control. Intervening in the physical brain in cases of clear physical malfunctioning is usually regarded as acceptable. However, when chemical, electrical, or surgical means of altering behavior are contemplated in the absence of any clearly specified abnormality in brain function, serious moral and ethical questions must be faced.

The wonder of the brain's executive management of all human functioning is clearly illustrated in both normal and damaged brains. When all is well, the fragility, balance, and specialization of the parts of the brain, with each component doing its part, speak volumes in praise of our Creator. The tragic results in impaired functioning associated with brain injury proclaim with equal eloquence the complexity and the wonder of our three pounds of pinkish-grey matter.

Going Deeper

1. For a comprehensive and compassionate treatment of both healthy and damaged brains, I warmly recommend all eight chapters of Gareth Jones's *Our Fragile Brains* (InterVarsity, 1981).
2. For an enlightening discussion of the uniqueness of the human brain, you will enjoy chapter 6 of Mark Cosgrove's *The Amazing Body Human: God's Design for Personhood* (Baker, 1987).
3. For a solid treatment of the debate over how brain and mind are related, see chapter 6 in Mary Van Leeuwen's *The Person in Psychology* (Eerdmans, 1985).

4. For an intriguing perspective on the brain's role in a wide variety of human experiences, see Michael Gazzaniga's *Mind Matters* (Houghton Mifflin, 1988).
5. For a Christian defense of the place of brain research, I recommend chapter 2 in Stan Jones's *Psychology and the Christian Faith* (Baker, 1986).

3

Sensation and Perception

In the area where I live, power outages occur frequently and for no apparent reason. A few months ago, we were hit with one just after nightfall. Suddenly, our whole house and the surrounding neighborhood were plunged into darkness. I knew exactly where the big flashlight was located—on a shelf at the back door. But negotiating the hallway and the stairs, and making it through several doorways without bumping into obstacles, was surprisingly tricky. How much more difficult all this would have been in an unfamiliar environment! Next time I see a blind person who needs assistance, I will be more aware of the challenge that he or she must face daily.

Even partial loss of sensory abilities, such as impaired tasting and smelling when you have a bad cold, proves to be an annoying handicap. But neither smell nor taste nor sight is our most critical sense capacity. It is difficult and confining to get along without these senses, but we can manage if they are impaired or even absent. However, without the stimulation of touch, many of us might never have lived past infancy, a fact that has been shown dramatically in orphanages, where infant mortality rates can be alarmingly high. Although the children have nutritious food and adequate health care, staff members may devote little time to caressing, cuddling, and rocking them. When the amount of physical contact and touching is deliberately increased, these infants' chances of survival improve markedly. Evidently, our Creator has designed us for physical contact.

In the Beginning

It is striking to realize that dozens of Scripture passages deal in some way with our sensory capacities. Frequently, these references are metaphorical, as when we are invited to "taste and see that the LORD is good" (Ps. 34:8), or when we are told that "the eyes of the LORD range throughout the earth" (2 Chron. 16:9). However, many others relate directly to the physical functioning of our senses, as when Mary's perfume filled the house with fragrant odors (John 12:3) or when Isaac's wife, Rebekah, and son Jacob capitalized on the old man's failing eyesight to cleverly trick him (Gen. 27:21–27).

You may be surprised to learn that when the discipline of psychology was in its infancy, most of its research was focused on the functioning of human senses. German pioneers such as Hermann von Helmholtz, Ernst Weber, Gustav Fechner, and others attempted to understand how our organs of sight and hearing put us in touch with the physical world outside our bodies.

One of the objectives of these trailblazers in psychology was to define precisely the relation between varying intensities of physical stimulation and an observer's sensory experience. As an example, imagine replacing a sixty-watt light bulb with a one-hundred-watt bulb. How much would the apparent brightness change? This field, now known as *psychophysics* because it examines the links between the psychological and the physical, still has an important place in the discipline. One major psychophysical principle is summarized in *Weber's Law,* named in honor of one of these pioneers in psychology research. This principle helps to explain why the first sugar cube in your coffee makes a huge taste difference, but the effect of adding a fifth cube (assuming you really like sugar) is barely noticeable.

Receiving Outside Information

The human eye working together with visual regions of the brain makes up a remarkable and efficient system. Our retinas, comprising the inside surface of the back of each eyeball, record tiny, inverted, two-dimensional images from minuscule amounts of light energy reflected from the objects around us. From the resulting pattern of neural firing in the optic nerve, the brain recreates for us the rich and infinitely varied world of external objects, colors, locations, and movement. The visual sense, while it is not the most essential for physical survival, is certainly the richest in the range of information that it provides about our world.

Our ears are no less remarkable, creating for us the ever-changing experiences of cheering crowds at the Olympic Games, beautiful symphonic music, the cry of a loon, or the reassuring sound of a friend's voice on the telephone. What we call our ears have little to do with hearing; their primary function is displaying earrings and supporting spectacles. The invisible ear inside your head miraculously converts the tiny air-pressure fluctuations created by sound waves into corresponding movements of bones and fluids in the ear. These precise patterns of movement result in complex sequences of neurological activity in the auditory nerve leading to your brain, thus providing your access to the rich and changing world of sound.

In typical explorations of human senses, taste, smell, and touch are referred to as *lesser senses*. Compared with vision and hearing, they occupy a much smaller place in our discussions, probably because they seem less important in most human activities. This view seems justified, for based only on the primary senses of vision and hearing, communication systems such as television can convey human experiences with remarkable realism. But consider how the exquisite taste of gourmet food creates a sensory pleasure distinct from any other, whereas the tiniest taste of spoiled meat can forewarn us about the danger of sickness. Likewise, the delicious aroma of lilacs in the springtime, freshly baked bread, or delicate perfume add pleasure to our experience. In contrast, the smell of smoke may be our earliest warning of danger from a fire soon to rage out of control.

As we noted earlier, touch is essential to life and to normal infant development. Although this sense is not well understood, it plays a crucial role in a variety of human activities including typing, reading Braille, or handling paper money. Touch is integral to the God-given pleasure of sexual intimacy. It also is closely related to our perception of pain, which, as we will see, is essential to our protection and well-being.

Important to our understanding of how each of the senses functions is the distinction between *sensation* and *perception*. Although the two concepts are closely intertwined, sensation comes first and forms the basis for perception. Our sense organs, each attuned to a particular kind of stimulus energy, pick up clues from the world around us and convert that energy into neural firing patterns that the brain can accept. We call this process sensation. We can learn a great deal from studying the sense organs of other mammals, for the physical structure and functioning of their receptors is often similar to ours. For example, the eyes of your pet kitten develop and function in ways parallel to the ways your eyes function. When we organize these sensory clues into meaningful experiences involving objects and events, the process of perception comes into play. In this respect, we are less like animals and are influenced by past learning, expectations, and beliefs.

The question of how much we can trust our senses is one we will consider later in this chapter. But first, let us explore the emotionally charged issue of whether perception that bypasses the normal human senses—*extrasensory perception*—is something we should get involved in.

Is ESP Off Limits for Christians?

Most of us are fascinated by experiences that defy explanation. Perhaps you have had a dream that seemed to forecast a specific future event such as meeting a particular person at an exact time and place. The dream had a disturbing sense of realism that was multiplied a thousand times when in real life its contents began to unfold according to your dream script. Alternatively, a friend or a relative may have called to say that she felt especially concerned for your safely at 9:20 last Wednesday evening. You reflect and realize that at that precise moment you were nearly sideswiped by an inattentive truck driver while you were returning home from work. Such experiences, frequently reported by people of all ages and beliefs, fascinate and trouble us.

In normal perceptual experiences, we receive information about the world around us through channels that we can at least roughly understand. In contrast, the mechanisms by which information is conveyed in telepathic messages or the special knowledge of future events is communicated are mysterious. Whether they involve the intervention of supernatural powers, they clearly go beyond the realm of ordinary perceptual experiences, and hence qualify as examples of *extrasensory perception* or *ESP*.

The subject of ESP is part of the larger field called *parapsychology*, for it lies outside or beyond the traditional scope of the discipline. Nevertheless, it has attracted a good deal of attention in recent years from both the general public and the research community as interest in extraordinary and non-physical experiences has mushroomed. Let's consider several aspects of the field that have captured most of the attention.

As it is normally understood, ESP is composed of three quite distinct but related phenomena. *Telepathy* involves transference of thoughts from one person to another without the use of normal channels of verbal or nonverbal communication. It is demonstrated when one person reports what another is thinking— for example, which of ten possible scenes that individual is pondering at the moment. *Clairvoyance,* as the parts of the word suggest, refers to clear awareness of information not accessible to the physical senses or known by any other person. This might be a randomly chosen fact contained in a sealed envelope or the location of a missing object. Finally, *precognition* occurs when an event that has not yet occurred is correctly predicted. In demonstrating this phenomenon, time relationships are crucial.

Each of these manifestations of ESP defies both common sense and scientific explanation. For those who believe in the reality of the supernatural realm, accounts based on the operation of either divine or demonic powers are often proposed. Some people believe that such abilities reflect God's power and providence whether or not those involved acknowledge the true source of their ability. For others, all demonstrations of paranormal phenomena are relegated to the shadowy realm of satanic influence, obviously to be shunned. Still others choose to believe that God is responsible for some apparent cases of ESP, and evil powers are behind other such events, depending on who is involved and who is the acknowledged source of power. Particularly among Christians, there is a heated debate over whether such experiences ought to be explored thoughtfully or avoided completely.

The Perspective of Faith

There can be no doubt that for the Christian, experiences that parallel those classed as ESP occur quite frequently. Many people I talk with can recall instances when they felt powerfully moved to pray for a friend at a specific time. Conferring with that person later reveals that he was facing a crisis at that particular moment. Presumably, in his knowledge of the whole situation and his love for the people involved, God planted the urge in a person with whom he communicated in ways we might describe as telepathic. Similarly, when I pray, my thoughts are communicated to God, but not through physical channels, for it is not necessary for me to pray aloud. As well, unusual knowledge of the future is not at all foreign to either the biblical record or some current Christians' religious experiences. Throughout Scripture, men and women of God (normally identified as prophets) correctly anticipated the occurrence of events that had not yet happened. The visions of Isaiah, Ananias, and Peter are examples of this. Thus, paranormal phenomena are part of a Christian understanding of life and human experience.

The Bible also contains clear and explicit warnings against obtaining or even seeking special information from demonic sources. According to Old Testament law (Deut. 18:9–12), practices such as sorcery, divination, casting spells, and other occult activities are expressly forbidden by God. Likewise, Isaiah 47:12–15 indicates that information obtained through sorceries and magic spells is useless. Although there is debate as to whether ESP is necessarily associated with the occult, these warnings indicate that great caution and discernment are needed in dealing with the issues.

According to the account of mankind's fall into sin (Gen. 3:1–7), part of the lure of Satan's temptation was the prospect of becoming like God and having special knowledge and insight that went beyond human understanding. This and other biblical teachings can be interpreted as forbidding humans to seek knowledge that properly belongs to God alone. In the minds of some, ESP clearly falls into this category. They see its basis in special insights involving a supernatural source, something we should not pursue. To do so would constitute an attempt to occupy a position to which only God has a legitimate right.

It should be evident from our discussion so far that the subject of ESP is a divisive one for people in general, and is particularly so for Christians. Virtually all believers would agree that occult activity is both dangerous and wrong, but there is considerable difference of opinion over whether ESP should be categorized as occult.

Some Christians see the whole universe and our planet in particular as a cosmic battleground for the forces of good and evil. They often conclude that any phenomenon not clearly attributable to God's power must belong to enemy territory. Since ESP-related activities, apart from those such as prayer to the true God, are not clearly of God, they must be avoided.

Other Christians allow for the possibility of natural human abilities that, even though they currently are not well understood, still reflect God's image and grace in human experience. From this point of view, ESP can be cautiously but openly explored by Christians as well as others. The reasoning is that God's powers are infinite and flawless, whereas ours are limited and imperfect. One example of this contrast is that God has complete and perfect knowledge of everything, but our powers of telepathy, clairvoyance, and precognition are fallible. They reflect a tarnished image of our awesome creator God.

Part of the dispute over this issue is related to terminology. If a person's ability to anticipate future events or sense activities taking place elsewhere is labeled as *psychic power*, it seems more dangerous than if these same abilities are called *intuition*. Most of us would acknowledge the existence of an unexplainable sixth sense that is not related to supernatural power, and would probably even report having experienced this ourselves. Perhaps certain cases of ESP are better thought of in this way rather than as psychic phenomena or occult events.

A Cautious Conclusion

I do not expect Christians to reach full agreement on so controversial an issue as ESP, but let me attempt to summarize the perspectives we have considered and identify some common ground. First, we can agree that Satan, along with his evil hosts, is at present permitted by God to perform remarkable feats in an effort to seduce humankind. It is a limited power, always subject to God's sovereign will, but it is a power much greater than our own. If we attempt to challenge Satan in our own strength and wisdom, we will be soundly defeated. Any area of study or work such as ESP, which might have occult links, must be approached with prayerful discernment and great caution. However, Satan's limited powers pale into insignificance when compared with God's mighty irresistible authority. Though still very much active, Satan is ultimately a defeated foe (Matt. 25:41).

Secondly, although there have been numerous attempts to demonstrate ESP phenomena in scientific and objective ways, these have not yet been successful. Typically, a person believed to have clairvoyant abilities is given the task of identifying which of several possible designs is drawn on a card hidden in a sealed envelope. Based on the number of targets from which the design was randomly chosen, it is easy to calculate the number of correct choices to be expected by blind guessing alone. Evidence for the validity of this form of ESP would mean finding a person who can regularly and consistently perform this task at a better-than-chance level of accuracy. Such a person has yet to be found. Therefore, many researchers, Christian and otherwise, remain skeptical of all ESP phenomena.

Another point to keep in mind is that in numerous cases when ESP appears to be demonstrated, it later turns out to be hoax. It is relatively easy for a sleight-of-hand artist to convince people that he can read minds or foretell the future. It is much harder for someone claiming to have ESP to demonstrate this to the satisfaction of a magician. Because cases of attempted fraud have been uncovered, extra suspicion surrounds all attempts to prove scientifically the validity of paranormal abilities.

Finally, despite the lack of solid empirical evidence to support ESP claims, it seems reasonable to remain somewhat open-minded. Personal reports of hunches, intuitions, and dreams that have anticipated future events, although they are not compelling evidence, make it unwise to dismiss all such claims as groundless. In addition, there seems to be no logically compelling reason to rule out the possibility of limited ESP capacity as a natural human gift. This ability can be understood as a reflection of the divine image in humans, a gift that, like God's other good gifts, is evident to varying degrees in different people. Whether this position will ultimately be proven true remains to be seen.

The Reliability of Human Senses

The value of our sensory capacities is openly acknowledged in Scripture. It is clear that God made the human senses, whether they function normally or with limitations (Ps. 94:9; John 9:2–3). They are evidently created to provide richness and pleasure in our experience (Prov. 24:13; John 12:3). While a life of faith goes beyond sensory experience (2 Cor. 5:7), our senses do contribute in important ways to the development of faith (Rom. 10:17). In addition, Jesus' ministry dealt to a substantial degree with the restoration of damaged sensory abilities, reflecting the value he placed on this part of our humanness (Luke 4:18; Mark 10:46–52; etc.).

The question of whether our senses are to be trusted is often raised. Intuitively, we regard sense experience as definitive—"I've seen it myself." After Jesus' resurrection, the disciples were invited to use their senses to verify for themselves the risen Lord's identity (Luke 24:39). We give special status to information that has been verified and confirmed by our senses, calling such information *scientific*. Psychologists are fond of reminding us of the fallibility of human perception, however. They often refer to visual illusions or point to examples of ambiguous or reversible figures such as the *Necker cube*, a three-dimensional blank frame that appears to spontaneously switch its orientation while we gaze at it. There is no denying that at times, our senses fool us.

Such isolated and contrived examples of sensory inaccuracy must not blind us, however, to the exquisite beauty and harmony of the senses. In our daily interactions with the world around us, our senses serve us extremely well and provide accurate information nearly all the time. This is often because we have opportunity to explore an object from different angles, at different points in time, or even with different senses. As well, the movement of objects often clears up any ambiguity about their identity. For example, an unfamiliar round-shaped silver object lying at the roadside may turn into the end of an ordinary pop can once you kick it or turn it over.

In his fascinating book on human visual perception entitled *Eye and Brain*, Richard Gregory (1990) argues an *indirect perception* position. According to this view, sensory inputs supply us with clues we can use to construct an inner representation of the world around us. These sensory data do not provide direct access to external reality; rather, they help us to check the accuracy of our perceptual hunches. Because these inner pictures of the world are based heavily on our expectations and past experiences, they are frequently in error.

Learning and experience play major roles in the development of perceptual abilities. Human senses are remarkably adaptable. This is demonstrated when courageous volunteers try to move around while wearing special goggles that either displace everything they see fifteen degrees to the left, or invert the entire visual world, or produce other novel sensory distortions. Although they are initially awkward, these people can learn to cope quite effectively after just a few hours or even a few minutes of experience.

Furthermore, we come to identify objects by sight, sound, or touch because of contacts with them in the past. As shown by the histories of people who have recovered sight as adults (perhaps after cataracts have been removed), our sensory capacities are relatively useless to us apart from corresponding experiences. In Mark's account of Jesus' healing of a blind man (8:22–25), the second touch of the Healer may have been needed for that very reason. With his newly restored sight but no visual experience with which to interpret what he saw, the man's sensory inputs were hopelessly confusing. His brain as well as his eyes needed to be healed. Clearly, our experience has a profound impact on the interpretations we place on sense data.

In debating the reliability of the information our senses provide, it is important to strike a balance. Those who wish to argue strongly for the subjective and fickle nature of human perception face a perplexing dilemma. Their claims for perceptual in-accuracy are based on scientific evidence, which in turn con-sists of information collected almost exclusively through these supposedly unreliable senses! If I am to accept their claim of the fallibility of human senses, I must conclude that science cannot be trusted either. But such a position is not reasonable in light of evidence that scientific understanding does lead to helpful changes in our experience. Except for certain isolated and spe-cific exceptions that are easily understood, our sensory appara-tus is remarkably reliable.

Every person's package of past experience is unique, and therefore each person's perceptions are to some degree differ-ent from anyone else's. These differences are most striking, how-ever, in either of two situations. When external stimuli that our senses detect are ambiguous, large perceptual differences are evident. These cases are both uncommon and of little practical importance. Secondly, we sometimes use the term *perception* in the broader sense of personal significance or meaning. For exam-ple, a rising rate of violent crime is perceived by one person as the most crucial issue facing our nation, whereas for someone else, this problem is perceived as far less serious than un-employment or the spread of AIDS. Applied in this way, how-ever, the term *perception* goes far beyond its use in the present context to encompass nearly all of psychology.

Returning to a universal human experience that is clearly a matter of perception, we now consider the troublesome topic of pain. We will discover that while pain is certainly unpleasant, we could not survive without it.

Thank God for Pain!

Have you ever met a person who genuinely enjoyed the pain of a toothache or a pinched finger? Most of us rush to the medi-cine cabinet at the first sign of a headache or an upset stomach. We postpone those inevitable visits to our dentist as long as pos-sible, not wanting to endure the pain such experiences might involve. As people get older, they experience more frailty and pain, and face the possibility of long and agonizing illnesses such as cancer. My father, now in his mid-eighties, remarked to me recently, "I'm not afraid to die, but I sure don't look forward to the process."

Our skin is our largest sense organ, weighing about nine pounds. Earlier, we noted how crucial the experience of contact and touch is for the developing human infant. Harry Harlow's (1973) studies of *contact comfort* in infant monkeys demonstrated that physical contact is important for the normal development of these animals as well.

In most cases, touch sensations are pleasant. An affectionate hug, a reassuring hand on the shoulder, or the welcoming lick of a dog's tongue are a few of life's simple delights. But woven throughout the touch receptors embedded in our skin is the sensory apparatus that enables us to feel pain. In fact, pain and pleasure, as they arise from skin sensations, are hard to distinguish physiologically. They are nearly the same.

The choice between our current pain-spotted experiences and a life completely free of pain would be an easy decision to make. Yet, surprising as it may seem, opting for a painless existence would be a disaster. This is the conclusion reported by author Philip Yancey (1977) in *Where Is God When It Hurts?* Yancey's conclusions are based largely on the work of a Christian physician, Dr. Paul Brand, who did extensive medical and research work with some of those unfortunate few who experience no pain.

Our skin provides the body's first line of defense against physical danger. The pain receptors in our skin serve to warn us of impending tissue damage and to motivate us to take corrective action. Based on many years of working with victims of Hansen's disease (also called leprosy), Dr. Brand concluded that the unfortunate effects of this condition result from the fact that it is primarily a destroyer of the pain receptors in the skin. He observed that Hansen's patients would handle hot objects or continue working with large splinters of wood embedded in their hands because there was no pain to stop them. Consequently, the damage that resulted was much more serious, for the abusive action continued far past the point that you or I could possibly have tolerated it.

The necessity for pain sensitivity is seen in people other than Hansen's patients. Those whose pain sensitivity is deadened by alcohol are much more susceptible to frostbite or even death from freezing when they venture out into subzero temperatures. We take for granted and are barely conscious of how often our pain receptors prompt us to shift positions, even while we sleep, so as to prevent skin damage. Paraplegics, who experience no such warning signs, face the constant danger of bedsores. In those rare cases when a person is born with a reduction in or complete lack of pain sensitivity, the individual faces perennial danger of injuring himself without knowing it.

The exquisite beauty and complexity of human pain sensitivity became clear to Dr. Brand when he set out to develop an artificial pain-sensing apparatus to replace the one his Hansen's patients lacked. However, in his attempt to duplicate the natural human system, Brand faced formidable obstacles. For example, our hands can accept without complaint the intense pressure of gripping a twist-off bottle cap, yet are sensitive enough to handle a tiny contact lens without breaking it. These challenges proved too great for Dr. Brand and his team. After spending thousands of research dollars and many hours of diligent effort, they finally abandoned the project. Brand's conclusion speaks volumes: "Thank God for inventing pain. I don't think He could have done a better job" (Yancey 1977, 21).

Every day, every waking moment, our senses operate almost flawlessly to keep us informed about the world we inhabit. Our senses of touch and pain, along with all the others, stand as a continuous testimony to our Creator's wisdom. Along with informing us about the world outside, they point clearly to the One who made us in his image. A heartfelt prayer of gratitude is surely fitting: "Thank you, Lord, for the gift of my senses."

Reflecting Back

In this chapter on human sensory systems and perceptual abilities, our key word is **windows**. Our senses offer us a spectacular view of all that surrounds us when we take time to notice. Rooted in physiological structures, our sensory systems translate the specialized energy forms they receive into the common language of neural firings. The brain, taking into account vast chunks of related experience, converts this barrage of neurological activity into meaningful events and experiences.

In considering the troublesome topic of ESP, we concluded that although scientific support for its legitimacy remains unconvincing, we should remain somewhat open-minded about these disputed phenomena. The possibility of links with the occult makes caution essential. However, the potential discovery of a natural human ability that goes beyond mechanisms we can currently account for is not ruled out by Scripture.

We concluded with a brief examination of the trustworthiness of our senses as sources of information about our world and a positive look at the crucial role of pain in our experience. The Bible credits God with the invention of our senses and affirms their value and importance in all aspects of life. In particular, an understanding of the intricacy of human pain sensitivity makes it clear that pain is a precious gift rather than a great mistake.

Going Deeper

1. For a sensitive treatment of pain in the larger context of human suffering, I warmly recommend Philip Yancey's *Where Is God When It Hurts?* (Zondervan, 1977).
2. For an excellent and thought-provoking account of the physiology and psychology of our visual sense, consult the fourth edition of Richard Gregory's *Eye and Brain* (Princeton University Press, 1990).
3. For a less favorable Christian perspective on the topic of ESP, see chapter 5 of Martin Bolt's and David Myers's *The Human Connection* (InterVarsity, 1984).
4. For a more philosophical treatment of the question of the reliability of human perception and the pursuit of truth, read chapter 3 in *Psychology and the Christian Faith,* edited by Stan Jones (Baker, 1986).

4

States of Consciousness

Several years ago, my brother Ron, who was living in Brazil, was involved in a serious traffic accident that left the lower half of his body paralyzed. To make matters worse, his kidneys stopped functioning a few days later. Because of a physical condition that became critical, he was flown home to Canada to receive the medical care he so desperately needed. In spite of this, his health deteriorated over the next month until at one point he was too weak even to feed himself. To say that all of us who knew him were concerned would be an understatement.

Although I do not normally recall my dreams, just before I was to fly to Toronto to visit Ron, I had a vivid dream that, to this day, remains etched in my memory. Members of our family were assembled around a table with Ron in an unfamiliar cafeteria. It was the first time I had seen my brother since his accident. I was amazed that he looked so strong and healthy, and I said to him, "Ron, you look so good! I was expecting you to be thin and sickly!"

Around the time of my dream, I was struggling to face the reality of my brother's paralysis and his weakened condition. As we finalized plans for the visit, I experienced a confusing mix of feelings, anxious to be with him, but also wanting to avoid the whole situation. Unknown to me, however, a few days before I arrived, Ron's kidneys miraculously resumed operation, and he began to make remarkably rapid progress. When we met, the scene unfolded precisely as it had in my dream. We were eating together in the cafeteria at his rehabilitation center, and I was amazed at how healthy he looked. Do you think this occurred by coincidence? Was it wishful thinking on my part? Did God engineer my dream?

Consciousness: Where Does It Fit?

Without question, one of the most significant characteristics that all humans share is *consciousness*, our awareness of and ability to respond to our surroundings. In the early days of psychological research, the concept of consciousness was at the core of the discipline. Nearly all studies explored some aspect of conscious experience—sensory activity, memory, social interaction.

A few years later, Sigmund Freud raised many eyebrows with a view of consciousness represented by his iceberg analogy. He proposed that the memories, thoughts, and feelings of which we are aware (i.e., the visible tip of the iceberg) make up the smaller and less important portion of our minds. In Freud's view, the unconscious mind, corresponding to the submerged portion of the iceberg, consists of hundreds of repressed impulses, memories, and conflicts too painful to contemplate. Although we are not aware of some of them, they nevertheless powerfully influence our behavior and our emotional health.

A few years after Freud presented his views, the behaviorist John Watson boldly declared that the entire concept of consciousness should be abandoned. He reasoned that because the notions of mind and consciousness could not be observed and manipulated scientifically, they could be safely ignored. For nearly fifty years, his thinking dominated psychology.

More recently, psychologists have resumed study of this important topic, for in spite of long neglect, it never went away. The cognitive approach (introduced in chapter 1) with its emphasis on mental processes created a natural home for the study of consciousness. Growing interest in mysticism, meditation, and religious experiences has helped to create a climate compatible with research on many facets of this topic. In addition, advances in brain research have prompted scientists to pursue the physiological basis for the universal human experience of awareness. Once again, consciousness is returning to center stage in psychology.

Varying Levels of Consciousness

Although everyone knows from personal experience what consciousness is, no one has provided a totally satisfactory definition of this elusive concept. To be conscious is to be alert and responsive, something characteristic of normal waking experiences, but lacking when a person is delirious from a fever, is daydreaming, or has passed out from consuming too much alcohol. But waking consciousness is not a uniform state either. Psychologists must try to account for the differences in alertness that occur when you strain to complete an algebra problem before the exam time runs out, or soak contentedly in your hot tub after a delightful day of skiing.

We all experience an important level of consciousness quite different from the waking state on a regular basis. We call it sleep, and it occupies about one third of our lives—a significant chunk of time. Psychologists study the various stages of sleep, which are marked by fluctuating brain-wave patterns, changing muscle tension, and varying respiration and heart-rate rhythms. A typical night of sleep incorporates several stages, one being *REM sleep* (marked by rapid eye movements), the state in which most dreams occur. Considerable effort has gone into trying to determine why we sleep and why we have dreams. At this point, we have several intriguing theories, but no confirmed explanations. We will pick up the fascinating topic of dreams and their meaning later in this chapter.

Psychologists also study a variety of less common states of consciousness that differ in definite ways from both waking and sleeping. One of these is hypnosis. People who have been hypnotized are still responsive to their environment, but in modified ways. Their attention is focused more on the instructions of the hypnotist and less on other aspects of their surroundings. As a result, they are more willing to tolerate distortions of reality and are more suggestible, although not without limit.

Another way in which people's consciousness is altered is by chemical means. Psychologists are particularly interested in the impact of drugs on both observable behavior and inner conscious experiences. Their specific effects vary widely; however, psychoactive drugs typically produce distortions in perceptions of time and space and changes in the way we respond to our surroundings. Reasons for taking these drugs include seeking relief from boredom, responding to social pressure, and attempting to deal with anxieties and personal problems. Perhaps some people use drugs just because they are illegal.

The altered states of consciousness represented by sleep, hypnosis, and drugs do not exhaust the possibilities. Other conditions in which awareness of our surroundings is changed include relaxed meditative states, profound religious experiences, daydreaming, and delirious states brought on by high fever. Perhaps one day we will have a more comprehensive understanding of exactly how these experiences differ from normal waking consciousness.

Having briefly sketched the major states of human consciousness, let us now examine more carefully one particular altered state. It is a phenomenon that has generated a great deal of confusion and controversy.

Hypnosis: Dangerous Game or Valuable Tool?

Hypnosis is a subject that evokes a wide range of strong opinions from participants and observers alike. It is by no means a recent invention, having been practiced as an art for hundreds of years. There are even allusions in Scripture to events that might have involved hypnosis or something like it. For example, according to Genesis 2:21, God performed rib surgery on Adam after causing him to enter a *deep sleep*. Other processes might have been involved here, but it is interesting that hypnosis is sometimes used during medical and dental procedures to reduce awareness of pain.

The whole topic of hypnosis is shrouded in mystery and suspicion, probably because many of its historical links are with charlatans and quacks. The fact that public demonstrations of it have often incorporated bizarre and extreme features has not helped either. So a good place to begin our discussion is to clear up some persistent rumors about hypnosis.

First, contrary to popular belief, a hypnotist does not have magical powers of control over his or her client. Hypnotized persons are not mindless puppets. Deeply hypnotized individuals are indeed more suggestible than usual, but there are definite limits to how far they will go in complying with the hypnotist's instructions. A substantial degree of willingness appears necessary for even a light hypnotic state to be achieved. Furthermore, people vary widely in how readily and how deeply they can be hypnotized.

Second, while debate continues over what hypnosis actually involves, its characteristics are not nearly as distinctive as is often assumed. Many drivers, for instance, report the condition of *highway hypnosis* in which they may navigate for many miles with little or no conscious awareness of making stops, turns, and other adjustments essential to safe driving. In addition, there are other situations in which people become unusually willing to follow the instructions they have been given, even though this involves doing something that seems foolish. These include participating in a psychology experiment or being an on-stage volunteer at a magic show. According to some experts, hypnosis can be better thought of as an extension of these experiences than as a unique level of consciousness.

Third, there is little or no danger of getting stuck in a hypnotized state and failing to emerge safely. There are no reported cases in which this has occurred. Instead, one either returns to waking consciousness spontaneously or passes from a hypnotic to a sleeping state, then awakens normally.

Like a variety of other human experiences, such as daydreaming or even ordinary sleeping, hypnosis cannot as yet be completely explained. However, we do know a good deal about how it can be induced. When people agree to be hypnotized, either for therapeutic reasons or out of curiosity, they are normally seated in comfortable chairs and are invited to relax and perhaps close their eyes. Then the hypnotist proceeds to speak slowly and calmly in a quiet voice, suggesting that their relaxation is becoming deeper and deeper or that different parts of their bodies are becoming limp and heavy. The evidence that the desired state has been achieved is seen in how these people respond to subsequent instructions from the hypnotist, or in how they behave.

What characteristics do hypnotized persons display? Their range of attention is considerably narrowed in that they respond to the words of the hypnotist but disregard other events. For example, they might ignore another person walking by even though their eyes are wide open. However, instructions given by the hypnotist to get up and walk over to the window and open it would likely be carried out promptly.

A second characteristic, one already alluded to, is heightened suggestibility. All of us respond to what another person says or does (except when we are in a deep sleep or concentrating hard on reading); hypnotized persons seem to be especially cooperative. They readily follow instructions to pick up a book, turn off a lamp, or walk around the room. In addition, they seem willing to engage in actions that we might judge to be foolish, embarrassing, or even dangerous. Hypnotized persons have been reported to reach into a beaker of acid or to throw the acid at a bystander. Curiously, however, people asked to *pretend* that they were hypnotized did exactly the same things. Thus it is difficult to determine how unique to hypnosis this enhanced suggestibility is.

An intriguing result of hypnosis is that for some people, suggestions that they will feel no pain are remarkably effective. While there are marked individual differences, for those displaying this characteristic, the potential benefits are enormous. Imagine how pleasant your next visit to the dentist could be! Reduced pain perception has been repeatedly demonstrated, but there is puzzling evidence that hypnotized persons are still aware of the pain at one level. However, this awareness does not seem to reach full consciousness.

A curious and much more controversial feature of hypnosis is the phenomenon of *age regression*. In an effort to help a person remember events from the distant past, a hypnotist may instruct the client to return to an earlier period in her life—perhaps age five. The person will then demonstrate the physical behaviors typical of a five-year-old child, including childlike handwriting, and may report specific memories from that period. Of course, without independent confirmation, we would not know whether this report is an accurate memory, a reasonable guess, or a fabrication. Age regression tends to elicit as many inaccurate memories as valid ones.

A good deal of research effort has been directed toward determining exactly what hypnosis is, but psychologists have not yet reached consensus. Some regard it as a distinct and separate state of consciousness, parallel to other altered states such as sleep or a drug-induced trance. This view is supported by the fact that brain-wave patterns typical of hypnotized persons are quite different from those characteristic of either sleeping or awake but relaxed individuals. In addition, some features of hypnosis such as reduced sensitivity to pain are hard to account for without positing a separate state.

Other researchers are convinced that hypnosis is best seen simply as a social phenomenon in which the individual adopts a cooperative and passive role. According to them, hypnotized clients show outward compliance with no real inner change. Because their criterion of acceptable behavior shifts, they engage in activities which to observers are quite unexpected. This leads to the mistaken conclusion that they are in a different state of consciousness.

The debate over what hypnosis actually consists of may yet be resolved through the insights that are gained from additional research. It is possible, however, that what we classify as a single phenomenon may be a collection of distinct psychological events, all of which share some common behavioral characteristics.

The Perspective of Faith

How are Christians to respond to the perplexing subject of hypnosis? A wide range of opinions are readily available. One concern that often surfaces is the possible link between hypnosis and demonic activity. In *Hypnosis and the Christian* (1984), Martin Bobgan and Deidre Bobgan argue that hypnosis has consistent occult connections. They infer this from the history and past associations of hypnosis, as well as from the fact that deception is typically part of both the induction and the testing of this state. They point to the controversial phenomenon of age regression as further evidence of the occult overtones of this practice.

The loss of voluntary control over one's actions is also seen by some Christians as problematic. They argue that yielding control of one's will to anyone other than God is inappropriate and potentially dangerous. It can lead to wrong actions, particularly if the hypnotist happens to be an unscrupulous person, and may open the door to subsequent satanic influence. To quote the Bobgans, "The human will requires more respect than hypnosis seems to offer" (1984, 36).

A number of Christian practitioners regard hypnosis as a tool that has a great deal of positive potential. Along with the deep relaxation involved, hypnosis offers a powerful channel of communicating with a person who might otherwise resist the therapist's suggestions. Consequently, it has significant value as a vehicle for constructive change (Shepperson 1981).

There is no doubt that this tool can be misapplied. However, we do not advocate terminating our use of cars or computers because they are sometimes abused. Neither should we abandon hypnosis as a therapeutic tool. In fact, some have argued that Jesus' advice to become "like little children" is compatible with the main characteristics of hypnosis. In both conditions, people are more open, trusting, and suggestible, and less critical, as they are in the midst of spiritual experiences such as meditation and prayer. To quote Matheson, "If hypnosis can escape its association with evil and the occult, it may provide a productive avenue for the understanding of religious experiences" (1979, 20).

Why do we observe such a spectrum of opinion on this topic among believers, all claiming allegiance to the historic Christian faith? One factor is almost certainly awareness of and exposure to the realm of the occult. If people have experienced demonic influences in their own lives or have observed them in the lives of others, this will certainly have its impact. They will consequently be wary of any practice that seems even remotely connected to the occult, having observed directly the havoc it creates.

In addition, one's assessment of hypnosis grows out of direct exposure to it. Contrast the following two Christians. One has observed hypnosis used as a form of entertainment, accompanied by public demonstrations of bizarre behaviors that serve no useful purpose. Claims made for the powers of the hypnotist are extensive and alarming. The second has seen the sensitive and cautious use of this tool as a means of deliverance for someone who has long struggled with severe anxieties or an enslaving habit. In this individual's experience, hypnosis is a valuable tool for healing and restoration. Each Christian forms an opinion based on the information available. Even more compelling is personal experience—perhaps of ruin due to demonic oppression or healing and relief brought about through hypnosis.

Maintaining a Balance

Hypnosis is a phenomenon that we do not yet fully understand, nor can we adequately account for its effects. In such cases, we are prone to invent supernatural explanations. Since hypnosis is widely practiced by non-Christians, the involvement of demonic influences seems to be a reasonable assumption. But a supernatural explanation of hypnosis is only one view. Because one can learn to hypnotize oneself, and because some people cannot be deeply hypnotized at all, we may be dealing with a natural human capacity that is intrinsically neither good nor evil. In fact, hypnosis has been shown to be a skill that can be developed with practice.

The possible dangers attached to hypnosis are real and should not be ignored. At the least, a person seems more susceptible to influence when hypnotized than when in a normal state of consciousness. Therefore, if a hypnotist has malevolent purposes, these may be more readily achieved through this means. One would be well advised to undergo hypnosis only with someone who is known to be trustworthy. In addition, the possibility of occult influences should not be taken lightly. It is always appropriate to be alert to the devil's schemes.

The fact that an experience brings with it the potential for abuse should not blind us to its value, however. Constructive clinical applications of this technique include treating psychological problems such as extreme anxiety or stuttering, facilitating proper distribution of blood throughout the body, and alleviating pain. It should be noted that hypnosis in itself has no therapeutic benefit. It needs to be used as an adjunct to other medical or clinical procedures. In that context, however, its benefits can be substantial.

The best attitude for Christians to hold with respect to hypnosis seems to be one of both cautious discernment and moderate openness. If this experience brings the threat of satanic influence, our safety is surely not in our own wisdom or will power, but in God's ability to guard us from the enemy. A spirit of prayerful and expectant dependence on God will help to prevent excesses or abuses in this intriguing dimension of human experience.

Having explored a range of perspectives on the controversial topic of hypnosis, we now turn our attention to something that everyone knows from direct experience. On a nightly basis, each of us enters the mysterious and alluring world of dreams.

Dreams: Tuning In to God?

From even a casual reading of Scripture, it is evident that dreams and visions have occupied a substantial place in the unfolding of God's purposes for his people. No clear distinction is made in the Bible between visions, which normally occur in the waking state, and dreams, which occur during regular sleep. However, several significant examples of dreams figure prominently in the biblical narrative. One case is Jacob's dream of the ladder reaching to heaven (Gen. 28:10–17). A second example is Solomon's dream (1 Kings 3:5–15) in which, in response to God's offer of a gift, the king requested and was granted unusual wisdom to carry out his responsibilities. In the context of Jesus' miraculous birth, the wise men who had come to worship the new king were warned in a dream to bypass the palace of Herod on their homeward journey (Matt. 2:12).

In these examples, as well as in many others recorded in Scripture, it is clear that the person's dream served as a vehicle through which God chose to communicate. The function of the message was often to provide specific warning and guidance or to offer assurance of God's providential care. As such, the dream contributed significantly to the individual's spiritual pilgrimage.

Psychologists have shown a good deal of interest in dreams as well. Sigmund Freud proposed that rather than being a channel of divine communication, dreams provided significant insight into the unconscious mind. According to Freud's psycho-analytic theory (introduced in chapter 1), the unconscious contains impulses and memories that are threatening and anxiety-arousing. Therefore, it needs to be closed off from conscious awareness. One's dreams offer a relatively safe way in which the wishes of the unconscious can find expression. Without careful analysis, however, their meaning remains concealed in the symbols of the dream.

Although some psychologists have agreed with Freud that dreams convey significant meaning and personal insight, recent dream researchers have tended to trivialize the meaning of dreams. The mind-body position known as *monism* (refer to chapter 2) adopted by many contemporary scientists suggests that dreams are simply the byproduct of the brain's unplanned nighttime activities. Although we may place structure on our dreams in the process of remembering and retelling them, they are rooted in random neurological patterns of activity.

Other researchers take a more moderate position regarding the meaning and significance of dreams. It may be unrealistic to regard dreams as the "royal road to the unconscious," as Freud contended, but dreams can still provide instructive clues to our psychological functioning. Systematic dream research conducted over the last few decades has made use of the fact that dreams occur primarily during REM sleep, a stage marked by alpha-wave electroencephalograph (EEG) patterns and by rapid eye movements. Furthermore, the content of our dreams is generally not random and chaotic. When research subjects are questioned about the content of their dreams, a link with the events of the previous day is often evident. Although their meaning may at times be obscure, the position taken by researcher Paul Robbins seems reasonable: "Dreams are useful in bringing up not fully resolved problems" (1988, 104).

Various Christian thinkers have picked up on the potential for self-understanding that numerous psychologists see in our dreams. Noting the prominent place in Scripture occupied by dreams, some scholars have made the case that we ought to pay attention to our dreams and try to learn from them. According to Morton Kelsey's *God, Dreams and Revelation* (1991), the bias of our culture blinds us to the significant place God intends dreams to have in our spiritual lives. He recommends that we take our dreams seriously, writing them down, asking God for understanding, recording the conclusions we come to, and acting on our dreams. To him, dreams provide one means for personal encounter with God.

Others see dreams as having value, but do not suggest that they normally indicate God's intervention. Hendricks (1989) acknowledges the prominent place of dreams in the lives of both biblical characters and church fathers, but argues that the dreams recorded for us are not ordinary dreams. It is clear that dreaming has been a universal human experience throughout history and that some dreams have special meaning, either as predicting future events or putting us in closer touch with God. However, it would be a mistake to conclude that every dream has meaning and importance.

Scripture suggests that dreams occur for a variety of reasons. Many of them fade quickly (Job 20:8), and often they reflect the stresses we are experiencing and little else (Eccles. 5:3–7). They do, however, make up a universal human experience given by God to us as part of the gift of sleep (Ps. 127:2). It would be surprising if one of God's gifts served no useful purpose. In light of the important place accorded to dreams throughout the history of Christendom, their universality across human cultures, and the significance attached to them by psychologists, it would be unwise to ignore our dreams. It is also inappropriate to demand an important insight from every dream we have, for each of us has thousands of dreams in a lifetime. Unless a dream is particularly vivid and memorable, we should probably not place undue significance on it. Even vivid dreams may be relatively meaningless. They may constitute little more than a reminder that we have unfinished psychological business to attend to.

Provided a Christian wishes to make wise use of the gift of dreams, the following steps are suggested:

1. Recognize that while God may speak to us through a particular dream, this is not the norm.
2. In order to take dreams seriously, write them down immediately upon awakening and take time to reflect on what they might indicate.
3. Adopt an expectant attitude. Dreams may provide useful keys to self-understanding if one is teachable.

4. Share your dream with someone else and ask that person to help you understand its message.
5. Do not be overly concerned about whether a dream predicts the future.
6. Since we know God is interested in our growth, we can ask him as often as needed for wisdom to learn from our dreams.

Reflecting Back

Throughout our considerations of consciousness and the various levels at which we experience it, the key notion has been **awareness**. Human consciousness defies precise scientific definition, yet it is an undeniable subjective experience we all share. Whether we are fully awake and maximally alert to what surrounds us, or in an alternate state in which awareness is reduced or modified, until we die, we maintain a degree of consciousness at all times.

The perplexing phenomenon of hypnosis was examined carefully. We attempted to understand why the mention of this topic generates so much controversy and what place it might occupy in the thinking and experience of a Christian. Although caution is appropriate for several reasons, the potential value of hypnosis as a useful therapeutic tool should not be overlooked.

We also explored the important but mysterious state of consciousness called dreaming. Although it is now clear that everyone dreams several times every night, whether our dreams have something important to teach us remains a matter of conjecture. However, dreams reflect an aspect of how God has made us; he used dreams in times past to provide insight, guidance, and assurance. Therefore, it seems reasonable for believers to pay attention to the content and patterns of their dreams and to remain open-minded about what they might tell us. Pleasant dreams!

Going Deeper

1. For a brief and positive look at hypnosis and its potential value, read "Hypnotic aspect of religious experiences" by

George Matheson, *Journal of Psychology and Theology* 7 (1979): 13–21.

2. For a critical assessment of hypnosis, read Martin Bobgan and Deidre Bobgan, *Hypnosis and the Christian* (Bethany House, 1984).

3. For insight into the range of perspectives that psychologists adopt regarding hypnosis, I recommend *What Is Hypnosis?* edited by Peter Naish (Open University Press, 1986).

4. For a readable discussion of dreams in the Bible, and how we can learn from them today, consult Lois Lindsay Hendricks's *Discovering Your Biblical Dream Heritage* (Resource Publications, 1989).

5. For a more thorough treatment of both theological and psychological perspectives on the meaning of dreams, I recommend *God, Dreams and Revelation* by Morton Kelsey (Augsburg, 1991).

5

Conditioning and Learning

A dozen times a day, we are reminded that behavior is powerfully influenced by its consequences. Suppose you have just heard a joke about Saint Peter and the pearly gates that left you laughing so hard your sides ached. You are eager to tell it to your friends at the first opportunity. However, despite your masterful retelling of the story, it elicits scarcely a chuckle. You will be reluctant to try this or any other comic act in the near future. Alternatively, imagine that in a moment of wild abandon, you decide on a radically new hair style. The change in appearance elicits a steady stream of attention, admiring looks, and comments such as "it's awesome." The chance that your hair stylist will receive more business from you in the near future is excellent.

The kinds of learning illustrated here have survive value, allowing us to adapt effectively to changing situations. In numerous ways, whether trivial, crucial, or somewhere in between, we adjust our behaviors according to the results they bring. Let's meet the man most responsible for clarifying how this happens.

Skinner and the Mushrooming of Behaviorism

The approach in psychology known as behaviorism (introduced in chapter 1) has for many years been a major force in North America. This is due largely to the colorful career and prolific writing of B. F. Skinner. Until his death in 1990, Skinner was behaviorism's chief spokesperson. Through his extensive and carefully conducted research, he helped to provide a firm empirical base on which our understanding of behavior rests. In addition, he was a fearless and energetic defender of the claim that individual human actions are powerfully shaped by consequences in the social and physical environment.

Building on the pioneering work of the Russian scientist Ivan Pavlov and his American contemporary John Watson, Skinner turned scientific concepts of conditioning and reinforcement into matters for dinner-table conversation. Not everyone in our society appreciates behaviorism, but certainly no one can ignore it or deny the creativity of the applications Skinner proposed. During the second world war, he was hard at work developing his plan for pigeon-guided missiles whose kamikaze pilots would be trained through behavioral principles to steer lethal weapons toward their targets. Better known applications include the familiar *programmed learning* modules, as well as various strategies for classroom control.

Whether we agree with him or not, we must give Skinner appropriate credit for his many achievements. Few if any other psychologists can point to the myriad of useful applications that continue to flow from his meticulous research and writing. Were he still able to respond, however, Skinner himself would maintain that he did only what his inherited combination of genes and his unique collection of environmental stimuli determined he would do.

Basic Types of Learning

Although he is America's best known behaviorist, Skinner is not the inventor of conditioning techniques. It was Ivan Pavlov, a Russian scientist, who identified the basic mechanism of *classical conditioning*, learning by association, that is now regarded as one of two fundamental varieties of learning. In Pavlov's pioneering work with dogs, the animals learned an association between the sound of a bell and access to mouth-watering food because these events occurred together repeatedly. People seem to learn many important connections in the same way. Shoe manufacturers attempt to link the success image of famous NBA players with their particular brand of shoes. Similarly, beer companies try to associate youthfulness, good fun, and the acceptance of friends with their brand of alcohol in hopes that you will respond appropriately.

The second fundamental type of learning—*operant conditioning*—has presumably been employed for centuries, but Skinner established its wide application. Operant conditioning involves learning by consequences, either pleasant or unpleasant. Because this form of learning works well with voluntary rather than reflexive behavior, it provides a powerful way of training animals to perform amazing circus acts, controlling human work output, managing the activities of disruptive children, and much more. Operant conditioning works in each of two ways. Behaviors we wish to encourage can be followed by appealing consequences such as prizes, praise, or social approval. Alternatively, we can discourage or eliminate undesired responses by following them with punishment—two minutes in the penalty box! However, as we will see, the effectiveness of punishment is open to debate.

It was once assumed that these two types of learning applied equally well to all creatures and all behaviors. However, the assumption of uniform applicability has been disproved. For example, studies of conditioning normally demonstrate that effective learning occurs only when the two events occur close together in time. However, many animals seem predisposed to associate a novel flavor with sickness, even though the nauseous consequences occur several hours after the taste experience. This atypical pattern has obvious survival value in protecting them from spoiled or poisonous food. Likewise, human infants appear to be biologically predisposed to learn language, for the ease with which they master it cannot be accounted for by conditioning principles alone. These are but two examples that illustrate both the lawfulness and the diversity of learning.

The story of conditioning is an important chapter, but it does not fill the whole book on learning. Another significant mechanism, one that goes beyond simple conditioning but still focuses on behavior, is *modeling* or *observational learning*. As Albert Bandura (1977) has clearly demonstrated, much of our learning of appropriate attitudes and social responses comes about as we watch other people and profit from their experiences. Later in the chapter we will discuss how this mechanism illuminates some of the methods of teaching and learning illustrated in Scripture.

The application of behavioral principles to human experience brings with it both benefits and concerns. Let's consider some of the issues raised when we apply behavior modification techniques.

Does God Approve of Behavior Modification?

Mutual influence is a part of our daily interpersonal contacts. Parents attempt to persuade their children to eat broccoli and to make their beds, while children seek to gain larger allowances or later curfews from their parents. Similarly, students make efforts to influence in positive directions the grades their teachers assign, while professors try to convince students to study more diligently. Interpersonal influences are everywhere.

Essentially, *behavior modification* is a refinement of these everyday principles of interpersonal relationships. It consists of a deliberate attempt to change behaviors in systematic rather than unplanned ways. The unique emphasis of behavior modification is on purposefully altering or eliminating behaviors that are judged to be inappropriate and strengthening preferred alternatives. Two examples will illustrate the range of typical applications.

Suppose that a young woman who has smoked for several years is now pregnant. She decides that for her own health and that of her unborn child, her smoking must cease. However, her efforts to quit by sheer willpower prove unsuccessful. If she were to seek the help of a behavior modification specialist, he might assist her in following through with her decision to stop smoking through *counterconditioning*. This strategy involves applying classical conditioning procedures to change her positive associations with smoking into negative ones—feelings of repulsion or disgust. This might be accomplished by repeatedly pairing the action of lighting a cigarette with a feeling of nausea or an uncomfortable electric shock.

As a second example, imagine that a competent third-grade teacher has a particularly troublesome youngster in his class. Young Nathan invests considerably less effort and creativity in completing assigned work than in pestering other children. As a result, he is increasingly unpopular with his peers and lags behind in his studies. If the teacher were to apply behavior modification principles in this situation, he might decide to ignore (as much as is safely possible) Nathan's disruptive activity and to deliberately reward his occasional periods of serious effort. This might involve catching Nathan doing his school work and immediately offering him a candy bar. Within a fairly short period of time, Nathan's productivity in relevant school activities would dramatically increase. At the same time, his inappropriate behaviors would decrease when he found their consequences to be less rewarding.

Although the behavior modification specialist's bag of tricks contains a wide variety of techniques, these two are quite typical. It should be noted here, however, that there is a good deal of controversy, both in psychology generally and among Christians in particular, about the wisdom and the effectiveness of a behavioral approach to influencing people. Some critics are concerned that a focus on external actions is misguided, since the real problems are deep within the human psyche. To other critics, the idea of deliberately changing another person's behavior smacks of manipulation and control. To these and other issues we will soon return.

Let's consider one final example of behavior modification in order to focus on the key issues that we face when this controversial strategy is applied. Practically all Christians agree that spending time studying Scripture is essential for spiritual growth. Yet many of us struggle continually with maintaining a consistent pattern of daily Bible reading. Can behavior modification techniques help us to become more disciplined in reading Scripture? Should these techniques be encouraged as a means of developing greater consistency?

In any behavior modification application, several steps are necessary. First, the behavior we wish to change needs to be explicitly identified. In our example, we want to change the number of minutes per day spent in reading the Bible. Our goal might be increasing it to fifteen minutes each day. Next, we would need to identify reinforcers that are currently maintaining the competing behaviors. Depending on when we intend to do the reading (e.g., in the morning, after supper, or just before going to bed), competition might be arising from the desire to watch a favorite game show or to get a few extra minutes of sleep. It's important to identify these preexisting reinforcers, because in order to do more of one activity, one must obviously do less of something else.

Next we would need to monitor and record existing baseline levels of the target activity. Here, we might keep written records for a two-week period of exactly how many minutes we spend each day in Bible reading. (Incidentally, I have found that the fact of keeping track often results in an increase in this behavior.) Suppose you find this initial baseline level averages three minutes per day. Now we have a reference point from which to judge our progress. It's not difficult to ignore our missed days, but we also need systematically to provide a tangible reward each day that we are successful in spending the targeted amount of time in Bible reading. The chosen reward should be something specific, personally meaningful, and easily managed. That might be your favorite snack (provided you were not trying to lose weight at the same time!).

In the early stages, it would be important to receive a tangible reward each day we meet or come close to our goal. However, for a variety of reasons, we should shift to secondary reinforcers (such as checkmarks on a progress chart) as soon as possible. These have no intrinsic rewarding value, but represent tangible progress toward the goal and help to bridge the time gap until more substantial rewards can be earned. For example, after meeting our objective consistently for a whole week, we might reward ourselves with permission to spend an hour at a favorite hobby or to purchase the compact disc we have been wanting.

The plan we have outlined, if properly managed, would likely lead to a dramatic increase in the time we are spending in Bible reading. What would the benefits of this procedure be as compared to other efforts, such as making New Year's resolutions or promising ourselves to improve? In the first place, our chances of success in the pursuit of a worthwhile goal would be enhanced. These techniques have proven to be effective in changing behavior, and in doing so fairly quickly. As a result, we would feel better about ourselves, having accomplished an important goal we had earlier failed to attain. In addition, we would likely learn something valuable from spending more time reading the Bible. A range of spiritual benefits might follow from the new behavior pattern, including a more meaningful prayer life and a keener sense of God's presence.

Despite all these advantages, you may still be uneasy about the whole idea. If so, you are not alone. Some argue that such procedures encourage a good activity for entirely the wrong reasons. Reading the Bible in order to obtain a candy bar seems cheap and almost blasphemous. It could be argued that we should do it purely out of love for God and a desire to know him better. God is concerned with our attitude, not just our behavior, and he will not bless a good activity that is done for the wrong reasons. In addition, some critics argue that providing extrinsic rewards (not directly related to the activity itself) will further reduce the natural inclination to carry out that activity (Kohn 1993).

The Perspective of Faith

How do Christians respond to the idea of applying behavior modification techniques? There is a lively debate over this matter. Roger Bufford (1981) in *The Behavioral Reflex* makes a strong case for the view that behavioral techniques, properly understood, are quite compatible with the tone of Scripture. At the same time, he readily agrees that some of the underlying assumptions of the behavioral approach are not acceptable from a biblical perspective. Mark Cosgrove (1982) is critical of Skinner's whole emphasis on rewards, and Mary Van Leeuwen (1978) has serious reservations about both the philosophy of behaviorism and its corresponding applications. Let us briefly sketch some of the major arguments on each side of this debate.

We should first note that the Bible places importance on both observable actions and attitude. Faith, if it is genuine, must be accompanied by corresponding works (James 2:17–24). Church leaders are to be selected on the basis of how they act as well as what they believe (Tit. 1:5–9). In addition, we are admonished to base our judgments on demonstrated fruit rather than mere words (Matt. 7:15–23). Clearly, behavior matters to God.

In addition, Scripture has plenty to say about the consequences of both good and bad behavior. God frequently promised blessings for obedience to his laws and reminded his people that departure from his commands would result in hardship and punishment of many kinds. (See, for example, Deut. 27–30.) Paul gives instructions that those who don't work should not eat (2 Thess. 3:10). The concepts of heaven and hell function at least in part as anticipated consequences, powerfully influencing our choices. Note further that the principle of social or environmental influence is assumed in Scripture. The Book of Proverbs contains many admonitions that reflect the fact that those we associate with have an impact on our behaviors (e.g., Prov. 22:24–25). Paul gives explicit instructions to others to "follow my example" (1 Cor. 11:1), and Jesus' ministry is replete with instances when he taught by modeling rather than by direct instruction.

Despite these notable parallels between behavioral understandings and biblical ones, several objections have been raised, signifying a need for caution. In the first place, tangible rewards appeal to our selfish natures. While they may be effective, they encourage an immature dependence on immediate gratification rather than on the development of self-control and the ability to focus on future goals. Thus, behavior modification may solve the problem at hand, yet fail to foster overall growth and maturity.

A second concern is that in applying these techniques, the focus of attention is wrong. The emphasis is on human effort more than dependence on God, on external actions more than attitude. In our example, rewards might foster a legalistic ritual of Bible reading that bears little or no relation to a humble desire to commune with our heavenly Father. The proper attitude is illustrated in David's deep desire, evident throughout all 176 verses of Psalm 119, to know God more fully through his Word.

In the example we have used, manipulation by someone else is not an issue since the whole procedure can be managed by the individual concerned. However, the self-discipline needed to follow through with this plan, including the ability to deny one's self access to rewards when one fails to behave appropriately, is often lacking. For this reason, it is more common for another person to take charge of dispensing the reinforcers. Does this individual really have my best interests at heart, or might the person derive selfish pleasure (positive reinforcement) from controlling my behavior? The possibility for abuse of these techniques is real. That alone should not disqualify their use, but it does indicate the need to be on guard.

Toward a Resolution

We have seen that behavior modification strategies can be remarkably effective in altering specific behaviors, including religious practices. Nevertheless, there is a good deal of debate among Christians as to whether it is wise to apply them. Good arguments can be made on both sides, and consensus seems unlikely. Nevertheless, it is possible to account for the discrepancy in views and to propose a balanced perspective.

First, a distinction must be made between behaviorism as a philosophy of human nature and behaviorism as a set of tools used to alter specific habits. Much of the debate over the appropriateness of these applications boils down to this question of whether the applications can be separated from the basic world view involved. To some, such a separation represents compartmentalized thinking. However, the methods for modifying behavior were in use long before Skinner articulated the underlying philosophy. Many behavior modification practitioners, some of them Christians, probably operate with little commitment to a behaviorist philosophy. For them there may be no conflict between these techniques and biblical truth.

A second basis for differing reactions to behavior modification is found in one's perspective on the issues of freedom and control. Those who regard human freedom as the absence of external constraints on our choices find behavioristic emphases distasteful. From a biblical perspective, we can agree that humans are accountable before God (Rom. 3:19–20), and that accountability presupposes a measure of freedom. However, the environmental influence assumed by behaviorists does not necessarily imply total control, even though radical behaviorists at times argue for that. Clearly, the events and people around us do influence our responses, a position that the Scriptures support.

Skinner and the behaviorists have drawn attention to at least three significant truths that Christians can affirm. First, although behaviors can never be a means of earning God's favor, they are nevertheless important to him. Our observable actions should continually reflect our gratitude to him for his grace, mercy, and providential care. Second, the consequences of our actions have powerful influences on us. Clearly, the concepts of reward and punishment are found frequently in the Bible. Finally, while we do make choices and are held accountable for them, the constraints on these choices, both from within us and from the external environment, are significant. God is entirely free to do as he pleases; our capacity for free choice is real but limited. In this respect, we reflect in an imperfect way the image of our Creator.

In conclusion, there is a legitimate place for behavioral techniques, provided they are used to encourage appropriate actions that honor God. However, we should remember that our dependency is ultimately on God. Behavior modification must be regarded as a temporary bridge over a particular hurdle. The bridge should be dismantled as soon as possible to guard against dependency on inferior sources of aid.

We have seen that there are different reactions to the complex question of whether behavior modification is appropriate for Christians. We next consider two areas of application in which biblical and behavioral teaching are mutually reinforcing.

Observational Learning and Discipleship

In the New Testament, the four Gospel writers each record a unique account of Jesus' life and ministry. Certainly, what Jesus taught in both sermon and parable is relevant for our generation. However, he also conveyed many significant truths, not in words but by *modeling*—the way he lived before his disciples. The fact that he spent three years living in close contact with twelve men rather than recording written instructions is worthy of note. It suggests that the most effective way for his followers to learn was through a process that psychologists call *observational learning*.

Albert Bandura, the well-known social learning theorist, is usually credited with exploring and clarifying the concept of observational learning. Used interchangeably, the terms *modeling, observational learning,* and *imitation* all refer to learning by watching someone else's behavior. According to Bandura, an individual's behavior may be strengthened without that person ever receiving any direct reinforcement for it. This occurs because one observes someone else engaging in that behavior, especially if that person's actions lead to reward. On the other hand, if I observe someone being punished for a particular activity, I will become less inclined to participate in it.

These powerful principles play a major role in the learning of both children and adults. They also find extensive application throughout Scripture. When Jesus sent out his followers to teach and to heal (Luke 10:1–17), he gave them appropriate instructions as to what to take with them and how to proceed. However, the most important preparation had already occurred in the preceding months. The amazed disciples had watched Jesus heal dozens of sick people, feed hungry crowds, and even restore dead people to life. Indeed, the concept of a disciple (learner) implies opportunity to spend time with a mentor and to learn by watching this person.

Each of us finds that our teachers, both formal and casual, influence us in significant ways. We tend to adopt the attitudes and values of those we esteem, even though we may at times ignore their verbal instructions. The leader who says "Do as I say, and not as I do" is unlikely to exert the desired influence on others.

Observational learning is evident in other parts of Scripture as well. Paul poured his life into several others, most notably Timothy and Titus, whom he discipled both by word and by lifestyle. In various passages (e.g., 2 Tim. 3:10–11), Paul reminded others of their opportunities to observe the way he had lived before them, even pointing out the benefits he had experienced thereby. On other occasions, he instructed his co-workers to follow his example (1 Cor. 11:1; Phil. 3:17–19).

We have seen then that the power of models is illustrated in both psychology and Scripture. This influence is most effective when it occurs in close interpersonal relationships. In this setting, we pick up from those we spend time with not just specific behaviors but also deep convictions and fundamental values. Perhaps this is why the Bible urges parents to spend time sharing insights and values with their children in the course of daily activities (Deut. 6:6–7; Eph. 6:4). It may also account for why much of the teaching of Scripture is conveyed to us in flesh and blood—the examples represented in the lives of godly men and women. They become our models.

Punishment: Use with Caution

Punishment is probably a universal human experience. Whether it means a spanking by disapproving parents, a parking ticket resulting from failure to read posted signs, or a reduced grade on a late assignment, we can all relate to punishment. While we think of unpleasantness as essential to punishment, even more important is its deterring effect on unacceptable behaviors.

Parents and grandparents sometimes boast about the extreme punishments they endured. But in a day when domestic violence and abuse is all too common, society has come to view punishment with great suspicion. Likewise, some behaviorists warn that punishment is not effective in curbing inappropriate actions. In Scripture (Prov. 13:24; 22:15), punishment is permitted and even endorsed. How can we use punishment properly and effectively?

There can be no doubt that in the Old Testament, God used unpleasant consequences, often at the hands of other nations, to punish his disobedient people. Furthermore, in the law given to Moses, God prescribed appropriate punishments for various offenses, with the consequences ranging in severity from fines or restitution to personal injury or even death (Exod. 21:12–22:20). The purposes of the punishments prescribed seem to include elements of teaching, of achieving justice, and of deterring further wrong action.

In the realm of child rearing, the Bible also endorses the application of punishment (Prov. 13:13–14, 24; 22:15; 29:15–17). Other forms of teaching and discipline, including positive reinforcement, modeling, and encouragement, are strongly emphasized as well. However, punishment is presented as a useful and perhaps necessary tool for correction.

Apart from concerns about harsh and excessive punishment that may border on abuse, psychological research identifies several limitations associated with even the moderate use of punishment. To understand them, imagine that due to her parents' safety concerns, an enthusiastic three-year-old girl is spanked for riding her tricycle down the driveway and out onto the street. One unfortunate side effect would likely be that the child would be less inclined to ride her trike anywhere. Alternatively, she might learn to ride in the street only when Mom is not watching, or to develop a generalized fear of and dislike for her parents. Depending on how severe the spanking was and how eager she was to ride on the street, she might avoid the street for a day or two. Thereafter, she would probably return to her earlier habits. All of these unintended consequences of punishment represent ways in which it is only partially effective as a means of controlling behavior.

James Dobson, author of *Dare to Discipline* (1970), discusses many behavioral principles of child training. He advocates liberal doses of positive reinforcement and restricted use of physical punishment. He does not agree, however, that punishment is to be completely avoided by parents. Rather he recommends that they reserve physical punishments, especially spanking, for cases of willful, defiant disregard for clearly stated rules. Thus, spanking a child too young to understand our wishes, or punishing for an accident caused by clumsiness, would in Dobson's view not be appropriate.

Can the biblical endorsement of punishment in child training be reconciled with psychologists' concerns about the dangers and ineffectiveness of this practice? I believe that it can. First, we need to understand that biblical teaching regarding parents' loving care for the children God has entrusted to them assumes that punishment occurs within a context of acceptance, affirmation, and security. Second, parents should always administer punishment out of concern for the child's welfare, rather than out of anger or a desire for revenge. Finally, fathers are warned in Ephesians 6:4 to avoid exasperating their children. Vindictive or capricious punishment will certainly bring frustration and confusion. We must never treat children in this manner.

Effective discipline will on occasion include unpleasant consequences for inappropriate behaviors, primarily when other means such as verbal direction, modeling, and firm encourage-ment do not work. It will be administered promptly and con-sistently after clear guidelines have been violated, and will cor-respond as closely as possible to the nature and seriousness of the misdemeanor. Also, it will be accompanied by explanation and teaching about the desired behavior as well as generous reinforcement when that occurs. In no case will punishment be carried out in front of peers or involve withdrawal of parental love and acceptance. A child's sense of value and worth must always be carefully guarded.

Reflecting Back

In our discussion of conditioning and learning, the central concept has been **behavior change**. Behavioral psychologists seek to understand the impact the physical and social envi-ronment has in shaping our choices and actions. Through clas-sical conditioning, we can often alter automatic or reflexive behaviors as we acquire new associations. Freely chosen actions are heavily influenced by their consequences, the mech-anism of operant conditioning. In addition, we learn and apply what we observe others do, an important principle known as modeling.

In considering the appropriateness of behavior modifica-tion procedures, we came face to face with widely applied techniques for altering specific behaviors. We noted that while these methods are effective in producing a noticeable change, this benefit may come at the cost of unhealthy dependency on external factors. They may also carry a risk of unwelcome manipulation.

Finally, we explored two areas in which biblical patterns and psychological research can enlighten each other. Much signifi-cant learning of behavior, values, and attitudes comes about through the observational learning described and clarified by Bandura, but earlier applied by Jesus and other Bible charac-ters. We also attempted an answer to the question of how pun-ishment can be employed so as to bring the maximum benefit and minimum harm for those involved.

Going Deeper

1. For an excellent critique of behaviorist philosophy and applications, consult "The behaviorist bandwagon and body of Christ" by Mary Van Leeuwen, *Crux* 14 (1978): 3–28.
2. For a thorough and positive assessment of a variety of behavioral concepts and applications, see Roger Bufford's *The Human Reflex* (Harper and Row, 1981).
3. For a disturbing reminder of the dangers of excessive use of positive reinforcement, read Alfie Kohn's *Punished by Rewards* (Houghton Mifflin, 1993).
4. For a general treatment of current behavioral thinking, consult Howard Rachlin's *Introduction to Modern Behaviorism* (Freeman, 1991).
5. For a guide to thoughtful reflection on the life and work of B. F. Skinner, I recommend Mark Cosgrove's *B. F. Skinner's Behaviorism: An Analysis* (Zondervan, 1982).

6

Memory, Thought, and Intelligence

One evening a few weeks ago, I was getting ready to go hear a guest speaker at our church. In the midst of my preparations, I suddenly realized that my spectacles were not in their normal location—on my face. However, I had no recollection of when or where they had been removed. Being somewhat nearsighted, I find it tricky to start looking for my glasses when I'm not wearing them. Unfortunately, I was home alone at the time, which meant I could neither solicit assistance in my plight nor blame anyone but myself for their mysterious disappearance. Making a determined effort to locate them, I checked in all the likely places where they might be, but without success. I had to settle for an old and rather uncomfortable contact lens that left my vision only marginally improved.

Perhaps you can identify with my distressing (and embarrassingly frequent) experience of memory failure. Our memories can let us down in some fascinating and frustrating ways. Efforts to understand how we remember and why we forget constitute a major slice of the work done by psychologists who specialize in human cognition. Before surveying the range of topics included in this aspect of psychological study, let's explore the origins of the cognitive movement and identify its unique emphases.

The Cognitive Revolution Gathers Momentum

One of the most intriguing recent developments in psychology has been the rapid growth and expanding influence of the cognitive approach (see chapter 1). During its early history in the late 1800s, the scope of the fledgling discipline of psychology was broad indeed. It included sensation, memory, consciousness, reasoning, emotions, and much more. This changed dramatically some eighty years ago as a result of the powerful influence of John Watson and his behaviorist followers. He proposed that psychology ought to concern itself exclusively with observable behaviors. As a result, during the decades of the twenties, thirties, forties, and fifties, virtually all study of mental activity ground to a halt since it dealt with unobservables.

The cognitive movement first began flexing its new muscles during the 1960s. Behaviorism was gradually relinquishing its tenacious grip on the discipline, partly because of the changing tide of public opinion, but also because of the unworkable nature of its complex theories. At the same time, digital computers were gaining prominence in many facets of society, changing human experience in at least two important ways. First, these machines took over many tasks previously done by humans. More importantly, however, computers stimulated a rethinking of what being human means and what intelligent behavior comprises.

This new movement is characterized by two prominent emphases: a commitment to explaining complex mental functioning in humans and a fascination with the parallels between human and mechanical modes of processing information. As a result, terms like *encoding* and *retrieval* and tools such as flow charts have become standard fare in both our popular language and psychologists' attempts to understand our varied mental capacities.

Our Complex Mental Capacities

Have you ever found yourself in a group of people speaking a language that you don't understand? If so, you already have some sense of the mountain of knowledge required to effectively use oral language. Because it is both a crucial means of communicating with others and a powerful tool for thinking, solving problems, and making decisions, language plays a vital role in our daily experiences. Psychologists are attempting to understand not only the structure of human language but also the process by which children all over the world master this complex system so effortlessly.

Investigations of how we attempt to solve problems constitute another major segment of cognitive psychologists' work. Although animals may be capable of dealing with simple problems, the capacity to unscramble anagrams, prove algebra theorems, get around in a large city, or persuade a stubborn car to start are all abilities we think of as uniquely human. As we shall see, the development of sophisticated computer systems is beginning to call this comfortable view into question.

In addition, the topic of cognition raises fascinating questions about intelligence in both people and machines. Efforts to measure human intelligence also raise a number of ethical concerns: Is it fair to measure something so personal as intelligence? Who should have access to the resulting scores? Are IQ tests biased against minority groups? We shall pick up some of these important questions later.

Forming the cornerstone of all cognitive research is the study of our fascinating memory capacity. Despite the massive efforts invested, we still know very little about the physical basis of memory, although many researchers are convinced it resides in the chemistry of the neurons and their interconnections. We have made considerable progress, however, in developing models of how our memory system functions. The distinction between short-term and long-term memory is widely accepted. Short-term or working memory holds the current contents of our conscious awareness whereas long-term memory houses a myriad of highly organized facts and information accumulated over a lifetime.

Although human memory is fallible and is much less predictable than your computer's permanent memory, several important factors can substantially improve your ability to retain materials to which we have been exposed. Among the most powerful keys to better retention are creation of mental pictures, efforts to organize materials effectively, and use of appropriately spaced rehearsal. Students sometimes ignore these critical considerations to their peril!

We now turn our attention to a topic that raises fundamental questions about what it means to be human. This subject is machine intelligence.

Alien Intelligence?

For many television viewers, the sight of the humanlike Data efficiently carrying out his tasks aboard the starship *Enterprise* is a familiar and natural one. This fictitious character embodies the challenging topic *artificial intelligence* or *AI*. It is a subject of heated debate and an area in which Christians need to be better informed.

With the development of high-level chess programs, computer-assisted instructional packages, and exploratory applications in medical diagnosis, artificial intelligence has moved closer to the center stage of public awareness. Simply defined, AI represents a collective effort by computer specialists and cognitive scientists to develop machines that display many of the features of intelligent human behavior.

In some areas, progress has been remarkable. Few current writers would want to return to the days without word processors and spell-check programs. As tools for telecommunications, computer capacity to make information available in faraway places and at lightning speeds is astounding. Sophisticated programs known as *expert systems* do a surprisingly good job in selected areas of human skill, such as spectroscopic analysis and playing checkers. At our institution, a blind student's computerized scanner reads her textbooks and converts the printed text into an audible voice. These and other developments amaze us. They also raise some disturbing questions about our identity and uniqueness as humans.

According to some AI enthusiasts, there is no limit to what intelligent machines will soon be accomplishing. Although most of us think of these machines as doing only what they have been programmed to do, the development of *neural computers* raises doubts about the traditional view. This new generation of machines is designed to simulate the complexity of the brain, which derives much of its flexibility from the complex network of interconnections among its neurons. Surprisingly, these machines are not programmed in the conventional sense. Rather, they store away information gained from their own interactions and errors, enabling them to respond effectively when they encounter similar situations in the future.

Despite these exciting prospects, however, other AI specialists are not nearly so optimistic. In the opinion of these researchers, claims of progress are often inflated, reflecting science fiction more than fact. Hubert Dreyfus and Stuart Dreyfus (1986), for example, suggest that AI researchers and their spokesmen have an image to preserve. They want the public to see their field as a solid science that is progressing steadily toward its goals. In the opinion of these well-informed critics, the field of AI, although initially promising, has encountered three major roadblocks. These hurdles have prevented the development of anything beyond a highly restricted form of intelligent behavior.

The first hurdle is our inability to build common sense into a machine so that information it encounters can be interpreted in proper context. This has proved difficult for two reasons: common-sense understanding is based on a vast array of knowledge, but only a tiny portion of that knowledge is relevant in any given situation. Common sense is required to judge this relevance, so we are stuck!

The second major obstacle to building intelligent machines is the fact that humans often deal holistically with inputs such as scenes or faces, but computers must operate largely in terms of discrete features. Thus, recognizing a smile—something so simple any child can do it—turns out to be anything but simple.

The third roadblock to building a program that successfully mimics ordinary human functioning involves learning ability. While we continually learn from our experiences and hence go beyond what we have been directly told, no machine has yet achieved this in any practically useful sense. Learning is easy and universal for humans but next to impossible for a machine.

According to Dreyfus and Dreyfus, these three obstacles form a formidable barrier that threatens the success of the entire AI enterprise. Although AI advocates would like to deny it, progress in the field has not been nearly as steady as anticipated. Some lines of research, initially promising, have now been completely abandoned. Certain obstacles may yet be overcome through neural computers, holographic technology, or other means yet to be devised, but a curious paradox remains: Computers find complicated tasks easy, but apparently simple ones difficult. To some, this confirms a suspicion that AI is headed down a road leading nowhere.

Nevertheless, the field of AI raises a number of fundamental questions that philosophers have long debated: What is the essence of humanness? Is there a mind separate from the brain? What is intelligence? The difference now lies in the possibility of finding empirical answers through the development of machines that challenge or even surpass some of the characteristics we have long regarded as uniquely human. In selected areas at least, most notably *expert systems*, this prospect seems particularly likely.

The Perspective of Faith

What reactions do Christians looking at the field of AI have? In their informative yet disturbing book, *The Invasion of the Computer Culture*, Emerson and Forbes (1989) argue that the computer mentality is a significant cultural force. It is a social factor with which Christians must become acquainted and to which they must respond thoughtfully. They see the great danger of this movement, not so much in the accomplishments that intelligent machines can attain, but in the impoverished view of ourselves that a computer mentality fosters. They predict that for children growing up with sophisticated talking toys, the line between the human and the inanimate will be less and less clear. The concept of humanness will be increasingly defined in terms of what intelligent machines can do, leaving humans with a lop-sided and shrunken view of themselves.

Other Christian thinkers find AI developments much less alarming. Brain scientist Donald Mackay does not object to parallels being drawn between the computer and the human brain; in fact, he finds the parallels helpful in illuminating human functioning at the physical level. He does insist that thinking is a personal activity; brains do not think, and neither do machines. Having distinguished between the brain and the person, Mackay has no concern with developments in AI: "It is a mistake to see threats to human dignity in speculations that other creatures, whether naturally or artificially begotten, might share some of our capacities" (1980, 64).

Mary Van Leeuwen's position, articulated in *The Person in Psychology* (1985), is different. Having surveyed the evidence concerning AI, she remains unconvinced that this movement poses any realistic threat to our humanity. She argues that the reasoning ability that machines demonstrate is nowhere near the essential core of true intelligence, one of the reflections of God's image in man. Her conclusion is that in the future, computers will be regarded simply as what they are—useful machines. This position is compatible with the view of Dreyfus and Dreyfus (1986), who prefer the term *logic machines*, a term that they regard as a more accurate label for what seemingly intelligent computers are.

Why do Christians take different positions on the thorny issue of whether the whole AI movement should be ignored, feared, or welcomed? Certainly, this field is filled with much speculation as well as some solid progress. The line between science fiction and accomplished fact is not at all clear, particularly to the outsider. People's backgrounds and personalities may also bias them to be wary of technological progress in this area. In addition, Christians have not reached a firm consensus on what it means to be human, partly because the *image of God* is affirmed but not defined in Scripture. Thus, the apparently unique human capacities being eroded by computer developments may seem essential to some but expendable to others.

The Challenge We Face

Without wanting to terminate lively interactions on this complex topic, let us consider a few tentative conclusions designed primarily to provoke further discussion. First, we can agree that God has endowed his highest creation with remarkable gifts of thought, invention, and creativity. Therefore, encountering noteworthy human achievements like those represented by AI projects should inspire us to worship and glorify the Originator of all. Secondly, we need to remind ourselves periodically that life is filled with mystery and wonder. Although science at times removes some of that mystery, we can be confident that despite all the divinely endowed gifts that we humans possess, we will not easily duplicate God's work, especially our capacities for morality, responsibility, humor, and intuition. Thirdly, we need to both be informed about further developments in AI and to seek God's mind on this matter through careful searching of Scripture and thoughtful dialogue with fellow believers. In particular, we need to think clearly about the essence of our humanness. Those involved in AI studies, and to a lesser extent those of us who follow its developments with keen interest, need to check our motives and attitudes frequently. This will help to ensure that we maintain our proper role as stewards who must one day give account to the Creator of all.

Having explored the fascinating and controversial topic of AI, we now turn our attention to two applied aspects of cognition. In both cases, we will see how psychology offers helpful insights that complement biblical teaching.

Storing God's Word in Our Minds

In a society where Bibles are so readily available, few Christians find the task of memorizing Scripture high on their priority scale. The time may come when Bibles will be in short supply or restricted circulation, but that possibility is too remote to motivate many of us. Nevertheless, memorizing Scripture passages can be a rewarding discipline, one that offers significant dividends.

Although the Bible itself rarely exhorts us to memorize its content (Ps. 119:11 being one notable exception), we are frequently urged to ponder or meditate on God's Word (Deut. 6:6–9; Pss. 1:2; 119:15). Thus, memorizing Scripture should not be an end in itself; indeed, this activity could even become an idol. It is rather a means to an end, and that end is our understanding and application of what the Bible teaches.

In what way does the memorization of passages of Scripture facilitate or stimulate meditation on its content? First, in the process of memorizing a passage, one necessarily becomes familiar with it. Since the essence of meditation is a repeated mulling over or prolonged consideration of the subject, the two activities are partially overlapping and thus compatible. A second advantage of committing verses to memory is that we can easily ponder them during activities that make direct study of the Bible either dangerous or impossible. Some of my favorite times to reflect on Scripture are occasions when I drive alone, do routine tasks like cutting grass, or encounter unplanned periods of free time such as waiting in the doctor's office.

If one chooses to spend time in this activity, how is Scripture memorization best accomplished? Although psychology does not motivate one to memorize Scripture, it can certainly offer practical guidelines for achieving this goal efficiently. The principles summarized here are not limited to memorizing passages from the Bible, but they are applicable. (As an aside, it is preferable to memorize whole sections rather than isolated verses. This approach minimizes the need to learn the numerical reference information, something that is relatively meaningless and easily forgotten. As well, memorizing larger sections guards us from misinterpreting what the Bible means because we are reflecting on a verse in its proper context.)

The first principle of successful memorizing is this: *focus on meaning and personal relevance*. Numerous studies confirm the fact that memorizing nonsense or poorly understood material is difficult; something that makes sense to us is relatively easy to retain. Applying this principle means beginning to meditate even as you memorize. Be sure you understand what a verse says, and ask yourself what application it may have in your situation. Reflecting on the meaning of what you want to memorize will make the words stick in memory and will also start you toward your real goal of meditation.

The second principle is simple: *visualize*. Form mental pictures; see the scene or the concept in your mind's eye. Practically all systematic memory aids are based on mental images because these are particularly durable. Seeing in your mind's eye the "tree planted by streams of water" (Ps. 1:3) is but one example. Obviously, passages that are sufficiently concrete to suggest mental images will be easier to memorize than those that are more abstract. However, with effort and practice, a mental picture of some kind can usually be generated.

The third guideline is: *pay attention to structure*. It is important to notice the organization or internal structure of what you want to remember. For example, it is much easier to memorize

Psalm 1 if you notice that it is organized around the theme of contrasts between the righteous and the wicked. Poetic work is highly structured and is thus easier to memorize than prose. But in any passage, you can identify its themes and divide it into sections. This will help in understanding the meaning and in noting how the passage fits together.

The fourth principle is related: *identify and use retrieval cues.* Each verse or passage will have a core, and you can use a key word or a short title as a handle to effectively retrieve the larger passage. Often memory fails because we lack the appropriate cues with which to reach back and recover what we have learned.

A final principle to aid memory is this: *practice spaced rehearsal.* Rarely is anything adequately learned at the first exposure to it; repetition is normally necessary. But it is important to spread out the rehearsal, especially in the later stages of learning. In order for the material to stick in memory, review sessions should continue well after initial learning is complete. However, these may occur after increasingly longer intervals of time. For example, you might memorize a particular verse, then review it again after fifteen minutes, two hours, one day, ten days, one month, et cetera. This will ensure that a durable long-term memory has been created.

Foundational to all of these principles is a yet more basic and general guideline for effective learning of concepts and ideas in any area: *be sure you remain mentally active.* There is nothing more ineffective than hoping to passively absorb the ideas to which you are exposed. This applies equally well to learning the content of your textbook, the ten o'clock news, or Psalm 90. Our memories do not function like sponges that soak up anything they come in contact with. Instead, they are much more active, selecting and examining what they encounter, and relating this new information to the existing contents of our storehouse of knowledge. As a result, the further we go in exploring a given topic of interest, the easier new learning becomes.

What Does Your IQ Score Mean?

Many attempts to explore the differences among people's cognitive capacities involve *standardized tests.* The best known of these measuring tools are intelligence or IQ tests, so we will focus our consideration on them. But you should be aware that psychologists have developed measures of a host of mental and personality traits—creativity, honesty, introversion, religiosity, and many more.

Intelligence testing is shrouded in confusion and misunderstanding. Many people attribute an almost mystical quality to these tests, assuming that they somehow magically determine the absolute level of aptitude that an individual possesses. For others, the whole issue of testing is an emotionally charged one, for they are convinced that IQ tests are unfair, sinister, and destructive.

The key to reaching a balanced assessment of mental tests is understanding exactly what they are and how they are developed. In essence, any psychological test—the Scholastic Aptitude Test, the individually administered Stanford-Binet, or the famous Minnesota Multiphasic Personality Inventory—consists of a sample of behavior. Whenever we observe other people, we access samples of their behavior. Two features distinguish standardized tests from more casual observations. One is the fact that the conditions under which the observations are made is constant for everyone taking the test. The second feature is that we have standards (commonly called *norms*) that show how a large sample of other persons behave in the same situation. Thus, test users can make a meaningful statement about a person's standing on a particular characteristic relative to others in the norm group.

Although in a direct sense a test is a sample of someone's behavior, the purpose of making the observations is to infer how much of a particular characteristic this person possesses. The trait of interest is usually not observable. We infer its presence and strength on the basis of behaviors such as responses to specific series of questions in a given time frame. This is something that we can readily observe. There may be dispute over what a test is actually measuring (i.e., its *validity*), but the means used to determine the worth of a test is a pragmatic one. Consider an example.

Suppose we are developing a screening test for the selection of salespeople for IBM. The test comprises a number of questions about motivation, values, interpersonal style, and career goals, along with items designed to assess knowledge of the product they will represent. We plan to hire only those who achieve high scores, expecting them to be the most effective salespersons.

How could we demonstrate that the test has validity for selecting the best people for IBM? We would first need to test a representative group of one hundred or more potential employees, then hire them all and track their progress for several weeks or months. Using a statistical technique known as *correlation*, we could easily determine the extent to which high test scorers are also successful salespeople. The test is valid for IBM's selection of future employees to the extent that a strong relationship is found.

A great deal of careful work usually goes into the development of a standardized IQ test. Such a device does not magically determine your inherited mental capacity. However, it does provide a useful piece of information for improving decisions, especially those related to success in educational tasks.

In many contexts, hard choices must be made. Many students apply to a university, but only some of them can be admitted. There may be forty qualified applicants for a job for which only one person can be hired. A remedial reading program can accept a maximum of fifteen children at a time, so many needy children will be excluded. In these and many other situations, difficult decisions must somehow be made. Provided it has been properly administered, a standardized test can provide decision makers with an additional piece of information on which to base a tough choice. The greatest abuse of tests occurs when they become the sole basis for a decision, and other relevant considerations are ignored. This, however, is the fault of the administrators rather than a weakness in the test itself.

How do Christians evaluate standardized tests? In her discussion of IQ testing, Mary Van Leeuwen (1985) focuses her criticism more on the definition of intelligence than on the tests themselves. She sees our concept of intelligence as both culturally narrow and only modestly related to biblical notions of understanding and wisdom. In a broader review of standardized testing (Faw 1990), the present author argued for the careful use of these instruments on the grounds that when administered and interpreted properly, they enable us to make more fair decisions. Certainly, the goal of equity and justice is one we can applaud.

Others have made specific use of standardized tests in the service of Christian causes. One application is in the screening and placing of missionary candidates in specific cultural and interpersonal settings (Lindquist 1983). A person of a certain personality type can be expected to fit much better in a team-ministry setting, rather than in an isolated, solitary setting. For someone else, the reverse might be the case. The goal is to deploy human resources for the maximum benefit of all concerned. In this and similar cases, testing should not be seen as a replacement for seeking the mind of God in prayer. Rather, it contributes to the human component in the decision-making process. This particular application of psychological testing has considerable merit, and we should be alert for further developments.

Reflecting Back

In this chapter, the central concept has been **information**. Cognitive psychologists seek to understand how humans take in, process, store away in memory, and later use the information we are exposed to. Some of these uses include communicating through language, solving the problems we face, making difficult choices, and putting our intelligence to work. All of them reflect the majestic image of God in man.

In attempting to come to grips with the specter of machine intelligence, we discovered that some Christians see in AI a serious threat to humans' view of themselves; others anticipate that the fascination for AI will fade as seemingly intelligent computers become commonplace. The verdict on this important matter is not yet in.

Finally, we explored two areas in which cognitive psychology and Christian faith can be compatible. We considered principles of memory improvement directly applicable to the goal of memorizing Scripture. The enterprise of standardized testing, particularly IQ testing, was examined. We concluded that when tests are constructed, administered, and interpreted sensibly, the objective of facilitating justice is attained.

Going Deeper

1. For a disturbing and enlightening critique of how thinking machines are affecting our view of ourselves, I recommend Allen Emerson's and Cheryl Forbes's *The Invasion of the Computer Culture* (InterVarsity, 1989).
2. For a good consideration of the appropriateness of our western concept of intelligence, see chapter 8 of Mary Van Leeuwen's *The Person in Psychology* (InterVarsity, 1985).
3. For an overview of standardized testing from a Christian perspective, see "Does Scripture Support Standardized Testing?" by Harold Faw, *Perspectives on Science and Christian Faith* 42 (1990): 86–93.
4. For an argument in favor of the information-processing approach in general, written by a Christian, see Donald Mackay's *Brains, Machines and Persons* (Eerdmans, 1980).
5. For an excellent and highly readable account of how our memory works, consult Alan Baddeley's *Your Memory: A User's Guide* (Macmillan, 1982).

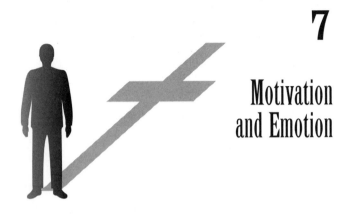

7

Motivation and Emotion

The atmosphere was hushed, almost reverent. Seated in orderly rows on the raised platform and appropriately attired in long gowns and mortar boards were 131 hopeful high-school graduates. It was evident to all in attendance that every graduate was keenly attuned to the evening's speeches, awards, and musical selections. Each one watched attentively. From time to time, a polite chorus of applause arose from the expectant group. When the correct moment came, each graduate in turn proceeded triumphantly across the stage to receive the coveted certificate representing the culmination of long years of classes, homework, projects, and demanding teachers.

As the program was nearing its conclusion, the principal made a simple statement: "Ladies and gentlemen, may I present this year's graduating class." Suddenly, all the pent-up emotion was explosively released. One hundred and thirty-one shouts, screams, and cheers were heard simultaneously and 131 hats were tossed high into the air. The celebration was about to begin!

A Tale of Fluctuating Emotions

Emotions are a universal human phenomenon. To be a living, breathing person is to experience the gamut of feelings ranging from ecstatic delight or blissful serenity on the one hand and deep despair or sheer terror on the other. Nowhere is this clearer than in the moving biblical account of the prodigal son that Jesus told (Luke 15:11–32) to convey the depth of the Father's love and forgiveness. It is a story rich in human emotion.

As the starry-eyed son collected his inheritance and set out to enjoy his freedom, he bubbled over with excitement, confidence, and anticipation. His father, with the wisdom of years and an understanding of his son's rebellious heart, must have been deeply concerned. But he still chose to let his son go.

Once the excitement had worn off and his resources were exhausted, the young man's emotions shifted to a combination of shame and regret, mixed no doubt with a good supply of guilt. Out of the depths of his despair, he pondered his options, made a tough decision, and headed for home. His father never lost hope, as evidenced by the fact that he saw his returning son in the distance. His persistent hope changed to compassion, followed quickly by relief and joy as he embraced his returning son. The son's anxiety and shame were quickly replaced with relief and gratitude at the acceptance of his forgiving father. Everyone agreed that it was time for a party!

Well, not quite everyone. The older brother's reaction was quite different. His surprise at the unexpected celebration gave way to jealousy toward his irresponsible kid brother and anger with his father for the hurt and injustice he felt. The story ends without telling whether the older brother's bitterness was ever resolved.

The Energizing of Human Actions

When psychologists attempt to deal with the twin topics of motivation and emotion, they face a formidable challenge. Both of these components of human experience are an intrinsic part of daily life, and they are inseparable from each other. Moreover, neither can be readily accounted for or neatly captured in a short definition. Psychologists' efforts have been directed toward selected aspects of these important topics, some of which we will briefly review.

Motivation refers to the forces, both inner and outer, that energize and direct human action. Some motives such as hunger and thirst have a clear biological basis and are fairly well understood. In both animals and humans, a special region of the brain called the hypothalamus plays a critical role in the regulation of food and fluid intake. Through its normal functioning, eating is initiated when blood sugar levels are low and is terminated when the need is met. Damage to the hypothalamus can greatly disrupt its regulatory function, leading to starvation or overeating to the point of extreme obesity.

Judging by the way they are exploited by advertisers, sexual motivations powerfully influence behavior. For humans, sexual behaviors are jointly guided by hormonal factors similar to those operating in animals, and by the cultural norms, personal experiences, and moral values specific to each individual. Thus sexual motivation stands on the bridge between physiological and acquired motives.

A variety of social or learned sources of motivation have been identified, including needs to affiliate with others and to explore one's surroundings. Particularly significant for students and many others is the *need for achievement*. This is a motive with no known physical basis, one that displays wide variations among people. Those with a generous supply of achievement motivation will expend great effort pursuing their goals and will frequently forego more pleasant activities in order to maximize their success in monetary, athletic, or academic pursuits.

The full range of human motivation is nicely organized in Abraham Maslow's *hierarchy of human needs*. Maslow (1968) proposed two major types of motivation—deficiency needs and growth needs. Deficiency needs include physical essentials such as food, rest, and safety, along with social needs such as a sense of belonging, worth, and esteem. According to Maslow, growth needs become prominent when deficiency needs have been largely satisfied. These revolve around the strong pull toward *self-actualization*, the development and expression of one's full potential in all areas of life.

Turning to the study of human emotions, we find a topic that has proved puzzling to researchers. No one would dispute the fact that emotions serve an energizing and motivating function. Just watch the coach and fans of a team when the referee's call goes against them! But exactly what are emotions and how do they operate within our total package of experience?

We know that emotions are multidimensional, comprising physiological arousal, subjective feeling states, cognitive interpretation of events, and observable manifestations in behavior (Izard 1991). Some theorists emphasize physiological aspects, suggesting that an emotion is dictated by the pattern of changes occurring throughout our bodies. Others see the role of specific brain centers such as the limbic system (see chapter 2) as critical in human emotion. Still others suggest that physical arousal must be interpreted in terms of both past experience and present context before an emotion can be evident.

Emotions influence us in powerful ways, often producing obvious changes in our posture, facial expression, muscle tension, and inner-organ functioning. One attempt to capitalize on some of these changes is the *lie detector* (or polygraph) sometimes used to assess the truthfulness of a witness's testimony. This device monitors various physiological patterns such as blood pressure, heart rate, and skin conductivity, all functions of the autonomic nervous system. If these patterns change markedly when a person is answering a target question, we may infer that the individual is not responding truthfully. This conclusion assumes that lying will trigger different emotions than answering honestly and that the emotion will be manifest physiologically.

Emotions affect us in a variety of sometimes mystifying ways, and we frequently have trouble managing them effectively. Would we be better off without them? Let's consider the place emotions ought to have in our daily experiences.

What Role Should Emotions Play in Our Lives?

Emotions are prominent throughout the pages of Scripture and particularly in the life of Christ. During his earthly existence, Jesus experienced a range of feelings including anger (Mark 3:5), sorrow (John 11:35), and distress (Luke 22:44). He was often moved with compassion (Matt. 9:36; 15:32), and even yet has great empathy for his people (Heb. 4:15). In all that the cross represented, he experienced both shame and joy (Heb. 12:2).

Likewise, God is described in Scripture as feeling both anger (Num. 25:3; Ps. 7:11; Rev. 19:5) and jealousy (Exod. 20:5; Ps. 79:5). Love is such a prominent attribute of God that it is synonymous with who he is (1 John 4:16). In the story of the prodigal son, the father (who represents God) experienced a wide range of emotions. In addition, practically every emotion we might name is identified and illustrated in the lives of Bible characters. The psalms are particularly rich in their expression of the emotional side of human experience.

Since a range of emotional states is intrinsic to the very nature of God, it should not be surprising that this aspect of life plays a prominent role in his image-bearers. But despite the fact that emotions are always with us, Christians have been reluctant to acknowledge their legitimacy, and psychologists have been slow to study emotions systematically. For years, the emotional dimension of our humanity has taken a back seat to the faculties of reason and of will. Emotions have been blamed for many of the problems common to human experience. This may help explain why investigations of this topic have focused primarily on negative emotions such as anger, fear, and guilt.

Defining what we mean by the term *emotion* is no small task, even though emotions are a familiar part of ordinary experience. We can quite readily specify what is involved in a particular emotion—fear, surprise, or relief—but the meaning of emotions in general is hard to nail down. In referring to the major components involved, Reeve colorfully describes emotions as "the maestro for the group of subjective, physiological, functional and expressive musicians that together produce an organized symphony of experience" (1992, 341).

To date, there exists no comprehensive theory of emotion. We need to understand the components of emotional experience more clearly in order to precisely define the global concept. In the meantime, researchers continue to debate whether physiology can be regarded as primary, or whether cognitions comprise the essence of emotion. It appears at this point that both elements work closely together, perhaps in a chicken-and-egg cycle.

Is there a limited set of basic human emotions? According to those who study the corresponding facial expressions, six distinct emotions can be readily identified in any culture. They are happiness, surprise, fear, anger, disgust, and sadness. Differential emotions theorists (Izard 1991) suggest that there are ten distinct emotions, each distinguishable on the basis of feeling states, physiology, expression, and behavior. However, our usual experience of these emotions is that they occur in varying intensities (e.g., concern, fear, or terror), and that they often come in groups rather than in isolation.

While emotional states and experiences appear to be universal, their expression is culturally constrained. When we visit another country or interact with someone from another culture, these differences are impossible to miss. People in some cultures are more (or less) willing to reveal their emotions than we find appropriate; alternatively, they express them in different ways. Even within our own culture, gender differences arise in that men are generally not expected to express their feelings, except after a championship game!

It is a matter of considerable debate whether emotions should be given room for expression or kept under tight rein. Because of the explosive power of strong emotions like rage, we often fear the consequences of losing control of them, perhaps to our great embarrassment. Yet the communication of deep emotion is important for building intimacy in marriage and friendship. Besides, those who counsel troubled individuals frequently report that pent-up emotions, particularly negative ones, figure prominently in the creation of both interpersonal and intra-individual problems. Thus the free expression of emotions seems both valuable and necessary.

The Perspective of Faith

Although some Christians wish to minimize the importance of emotions, Archibald Hart, a Christian counselor, believes that we must avoid the assumption that emotions are incompatible with a life of faith. In his enlightening book *Feeling Free*, Hart contends that neither the uncontrolled expression of strong emotion nor the bottling up of our feelings is appropriate. He believes that feelings give life its sparkle and spice. We need to both embrace them and take charge of them. But trying to be in total control of our emotions spawns an artificiality and denies a part of our real selves. Hart argues for a balance between the two extremes when he says, "To avoid feeling is to avoid life! To feel too much is to destroy life" (1979, 16).

Other writers agree that both extremes should be avoided, but that for most people, the unrestrained expression of emotion constitutes the greater danger. James Dobson notes that we are often encouraged to express ourselves honestly regardless of the consequences, and that anything that feels right is appropriate to do. He believes that our emotions cannot be trusted. The correct approach is to take charge of our emotions rather than letting them control us: "Emotions must always be accountable to the faculties of reason and will" (1980, 6).

Why do Christians fear and distrust their emotions when they are clearly a part of God's divinity and our humanity? For one thing, emotions are a vehicle through which temptations frequently come to us. Without doubt, strong anger can move us to express hateful feelings or to engage in violent and destructive acts of revenge. Fear may cripple us and prevent us from acting on a sense of God's leading when he prompts us to get involved in kingdom building. The cruel and destructive power of lust is demonstrated repeatedly in the broken relationships that permeate our society. From the perspective of these examples, we would be far better off without our emotions.

In addition, the unbridled expression of emotion is often a sign of selfish immaturity. We may excuse children for failing to control their emotions, but long for the day when with growing maturity they will exercise greater restraint. Acts of heroism and courage often involve refusing to give in to the emotions of fear and doing what our minds tell us is right.

Throughout history, Christians have struggled with the importance of subjective feelings and experiences on the one hand and the objective truth of historic Christian beliefs on the other. The place of Christian theology has been to guard the purity of the truth of Scripture and doctrine. This has left little room for emotions. The priority that psychologists have placed on emotions and their legitimate expression may have confirmed theology's focus on doctrinal correctness, partly as a means of maintaining its distinctive. It is time we recognize the legitimacy of both feelings and objective truth.

The Value of Emotions

Our relationship with God is critically dependent on the truth of what we believe and affirm. The Bible conveys to us an objective record of what God has communicated regarding himself and his creation. This we must understand with our minds and embrace as a choice of our wills. But a relationship with God through Jesus Christ, like any other interpersonal relationship, is of necessity an emotional one in which love has a central place. Cold logic and sterile belief are no substitutes for the fervor and freshness of a love for God that encompasses our minds, hearts, bodies, and emotions. The apostle John's letter to the church at Ephesus makes this clear (Rev. 2:4).

We will shortly focus on the particularly troublesome emotion of anger and will consider how we might manage it appropriately. In the meantime, we need to recognize that emotions have a legitimate place and can have a positive function in our lives. Emotions are part of God's nature, and he has given them to us for our benefit. They provide life's color, its melody, its fragrance, its sparkle. Christian maturity as represented in the fruit of the Spirit (Gal. 5:22–23) includes human characteristics with emotional components. While the characteristics of Christ's life within us (e.g., love, joy, peace) are more than emotions, they clearly have an emotional component. Our Lord's own example demonstrates that a life of faith in and obedience to God is one rich in emotion.

Finally, it is worth noting that all emotions, even the negative ones, serve important purposes. Our fear can drive us to prayer and to God as we seek comfort and security. Our joy can sustain us through the difficulties and hurdles we inevitably find in our path. Even anger can motivate us as nothing else will to take action in seeking his kingdom and bringing justice to the oppressed. In all our relationships, as we communicate our emotional experiences to one another, we grow in an understanding of who we are as unique individuals created to reflect his nature.

There is no doubt that emotions motivate us to act. But other motives can be identified as well. All of them are important to understand in our efforts to effectively communicate the message of Christ to others.

The Gospel and the Gamut of Human Need

People display endless variety in what moves them—what motivates them to get involved. Only when we begin to understand what makes another person tick are we really getting to know that individual. One friend eats, sleeps, and breathes computers. He loves the challenge of a programming problem and is never happier than when he is sorting out something that can't be done. Another friend has spent nearly twenty years engaged in medical and literacy work with a small tribe of a few hundred Indian people in a remote corner of northern Brazil. She is motivated by a sense of calling and compassion that I still can't fully understand. Both these individuals are an inspiration to me.

To understand and relate effectively with people, we must know something of their felt needs, for this is what motivates them. In his helpful summary of the range of typical human needs, Maslow (1968) proposed the idea of a hierarchy of needs, which is represented in psychology and management books in the form of a pyramid. The framework of this hierarchy provides a helpful tool for those who seek to communicate the gospel to others.

At the base of the pyramid are the most essential human needs for food, shelter, and security. For individuals or cultures in which these are lacking, nothing else matters much. These needs must be met before awareness of higher needs rises to prominence. The place to start in our evangelistic efforts is to make certain that these basic needs are met—to clothe the naked and feed the hungry as Jesus directed (Matt. 25:34–40). It is noteworthy that the legitimacy of physical needs is frequently recognized in Scripture (Matt. 6:25–34; Prov. 29:25) and that a large portion of Jesus' ministry of teaching and healing was directed to meeting people's physical needs (Luke 7:22; Mark 8:1–10).

In the middle of Maslow's scheme are social needs for love, acceptance, and esteem. Awareness of higher-level needs is once again largely blocked by severe deficits in these domains of experience. One attraction of religious cults is their capacity to provide lonely and unloved people with a sense of acceptance and belonging. True Christianity also recognizes and addresses these needs. The Bible's most prominent theme is love. Humans' greatest need is first to experience the love and forgiveness of God, and then to know the love of other people. God expresses his love to us by accepting us as his very own children (2 Cor. 6:18; John 1:12). We are accorded respect and dignity by God (Ps. 8:5) and are urged to offer the same to others (Phil. 2:3; 1 Pet. 2:17).

The highest level in the hierarchy is the universal human need to find fulfillment and purpose—to develop one's potential as fully as possible and thus experience *self-actualization*. True self-actualization is quite rare, according to Maslow, and is enjoyed by a handful of the very healthiest people. We each experience snatches of this lofty condition in *peak experiences*, moments of bliss when we are fully absorbed in mystical contemplation, creative expression, or sexual union. Self-actualizers (and each of us in peak experiences) display godlike characteristics such as self-forgetfulness, timelessness, uncritical acceptance of others, and childlike wonder.

The relationship between self-actualization in Maslow's purely human sense and the discovery of meaning and purpose in finding rest in our Creator is open to debate. Though religious experiences of worship and awe are included in what Maslow talked about, they are only one of many ways of becoming self-actualized. The focus on the self seems directly opposed to the criteria Jesus laid out for finding real life and purpose, for he indicated the necessity of denial of the self (Luke 9:23–24). On the other hand, Jesus addressed our need for purpose when he promised we could have abundant life (John 10:10). As well, many of the characteristics of self-actualizers match the marks of a true disciple.

It is the experience of devout Christians who have very little of material resources and human support that God can meet all their needs. Certainly the lives of Bible characters such as Paul demonstrate this (Phil. 4:10–19). Nevertheless, God has created us with normal human needs and limitations, and we function best when these are attended to. Both experience and Scripture attest to the truth of this claim. Maslow's hierarchy reminds us of areas of human experience to which we can usefully direct our attention as we attempt to communicate God's truth in a way that strikes a responsive chord.

Dealing Constructively with Anger

Of all the emotions we struggle to manage well, anger is perhaps the most challenging. Think of a recent occasion when you felt angry, and take a moment to reflect on that experience. When we feel angry, we are energized, for anger prepares us for action. It provides courage, so that we are willing to face situations or people we might otherwise find intimidating. The way we give expression to our anger, either verbally or in overt behavior, determines whether it is a constructive or a destructive emotion.

Most commonly, anger is triggered either physically by factors such as pain or restraint, or mentally by the attribution of blame for injustice. Ideally, anger motivates us to rectify situations by taking corrective action. However, it also has the potential to lead to a spirit of hostility and hatred that can be destructive to everyone involved.

Considerable confusion surrounds this topic, and conflicting advice is plentiful. Some believe that anger is nearly always destructive when expressed, and should therefore be stifled or at least tightly controlled. But many counselors who observe in their clients the negative consequences of repressing anger—strained interpersonal relationships, psychosomatic illnesses, and even depression—argue that the expression of anger is good and necessary.

When we examine the teachings of Scripture, various examples and guidelines concerning anger emerge. The Bible contains frequent reference to the anger of God (Num. 25:3; Jer. 8:19; Rev. 19:15). It is evident that on occasion, Jesus felt angry (Mark 3:5). From this we can conclude that the emotion of anger itself is not wrong, provided this feeling does not develop into hatred. We are, however, warned repeatedly of the dangers of anger (Prov. 22:24; Eph. 4:26; Matt. 2:16) and are instructed to be "slow to become angry" (James 1:19; Prov. 14:29). These cautions, it would appear, have less to do with the feeling itself and more to do with the way we behave when we are gripped by strong anger.

The initial feeling of anger is triggered by an external event and comprises a mixture of habitual and involuntary processes over which we have little control. Because anger energizes us and provides courage, we may assume that our anger compels us to act in a certain way; however, this is not the case. As Carroll Izard puts it, "Anger prepares us well for action, but it does not command or compel us to act" (1991, 248). Thus, when we feel angry, we choose to either repress our anger or to express it openly. There are dangers in repressing it, but there are also risks in the unwise expression of anger. Choosing to vent anger carries with it the responsibility to do so constructively.

When Jesus became angry with the synagogue attenders (Mark 3:5), he "looked around at them" before taking action. When Nehemiah became angry with the injustice done to his fellow Israelites (Neh. 5:6–7), he stopped to ponder before speaking. The rule of counting to ten is a valid one, for when we are angry, we must make decisions about whether and how to express ourselves. It is easier to make a wise choice at this point than to later repair the damage caused by a thoughtless outburst.

In order to follow the instructions of Ephesians 4:26 and Psalm 4:4 to avoid sinning in our anger, we need to pause and determine how to express our feelings in a constructive and responsible way. But we should express them, for anger needs to be resolved. We must also remember that because anger is a powerful motivator, it can facilitate honesty in communication. In our anger we can find the courage to clearly express what needs to be said. This will be constructive, provided we take ownership of our anger and make certain that our objective is building understanding rather than winning battles.

In his helpful treatment of this topic, Hart (1979) points out that anger is most easily dealt with in the earliest stages of its development. He believes that unrealistic expectations are a common cause of anger, and suggests that correcting faulty beliefs through self-talk can frequently reduce strong feelings of anger. For example, I might consciously remind myself that the person who has just wronged me has been short on sleep for the past three nights and probably does not really mean what she just said. If we find we are feeling angry, however, it is important to admit this to ourselves openly and honestly. The best way to put an end to our anger is to deliberately release our right to get even, recognizing that in trying to retaliate, we will probably go too far. The Bible is clear that taking vengeance is God's responsibility (Rom. 12: 19–20). He can do it far more equitably and effectively than we can.

Jesus' supreme example to us in responding to the injustices he faced was to forgive his enemies even as he suffered painfully on the cross (Luke 23:34). Once our anger has become fully developed, forgiveness is the only adequate way to resolve it. This is not a natural human response, for our sinful nature and desire to get even runs very deep. Nevertheless, for the sake of our relationships with others and our own psychological health, we really have no other good options. God has forgiven us, and he expects us to pass it on.

The emotion of anger is an intrinsic part of our humanness. It has potential for frightful destruction as well as for tremendous benefit, depending on how it is managed. Although the initial rush of feeling probably happens to us with little choice or control on our part, the next steps we take are much more deliberate. We can often diffuse the anger in its earliest stages by correcting faulty expectations. As it progresses, we can grit our teeth and deny our feelings, give full expression to our desire for revenge in destructive words or actions, or pause briefly and choose an effective way to channel this energy. When anger evolves into smoldering feelings of hostility or overtly injurious actions, it will be resolved only when we seek God's forgiveness for our sin and his grace to extend forgiveness to those who have wronged us. Easy to do? By no means. Worth the cost? Absolutely.

Reflecting Back

Our discussion of the complex topics of motivation and emotion have centered around the idea of **needs**. Motives are usually rooted in needs, either innate ones such as thirst or learned needs such as the desire to achieve success. Emotions are often triggered by events around us, such as when access to the usual means of meeting our needs is blocked. Our desire for fairness and equity, when it is violated, can lead to anger.

We debated the place that emotions should have in a person's life. Some see emotions mainly as a liability to be overcome, while others regard them as gifts from God to be entered into and appreciated. Our conclusion is that our emotions are a mixed blessing. They do present challenges, but are essential to our humanity and provide life with an additional dimension of richness, variety, and fulfillment.

We noted some parallels between Maslow's hierarchy of motives and biblical affirmations of legitimate human needs. Effective proclamation of God's truth will involve responding to all levels of need. Finally, we explored ways in which anger can be managed, concluding that when properly channelled, it has great potential for positive and constructive communication.

Going Deeper

1. For a comprehensive and up to date discussion of this entire subject, I recommend *Understanding Motivation and Emotion* by Johnmarshall Reeve (Harcourt Brace, 1992).
2. For a stimulating and readable treatment of anger and other troublesome emotions, you will enjoy Archibald Hart's *Feeling Free* (Revell, 1979).
3. For more insight into the fascinating concept of self-actualization, consult Abraham Maslow's *Toward a Psychology of Being* (Van Nostrand Reinhold, 1968).
4. For some thoughtful reflections of how emotions relate to the fruit of the Spirit, read chapter 4 in Stan Jones's *Psychology and the Christian Faith* (Baker, 1986).

8

Development Through the Lifespan

Returning to my home community for a visit recently, I had a shocking experience. When I entered my parents' church with them, I was approached by a man in his early twenties whom I did not recognize. He introduced himself as my second cousin Wes, a person I clearly remembered but had not seen in many years. My surprise was not that he was attending church, or even that he recognized me after more than fifteen years. In fact, I was flattered. What shocked and puzzled me was the discrepancy between the poised, mature gentleman standing before me and the lingering image of a timid, reticent lad of about four—an image frozen in my memory. How had he suddenly become a mature young man? How could he be finished with four years of theological studies and nearly ready to assume pastoral duties? Changes of this magnitude ought not to occur overnight. But as my father-in-law is fond of saying, "Time marches on!"

Forever Changing, Always the Same

Human experience consists of a blend of constancy and flux. Some things never change—Uncle Henry's mischievous and ready grin, Aunt Muriel's unique expression "for the love of Peter!" or cousin Matt's firm handshake. If it were not for constancy, we would all be strangers again after each fond farewell. But as time passes, people do change, sometimes in dramatic ways. It's more obvious of course with children and infants—babies change in both appearance and capabilities practically every day. Toddlers learn to walk and soon to run, making their parents run as well. Preschoolers suddenly master two-wheeled bicycles or stay overnight with a friend for the first time. The film companies are correct—we need to "capture the moment," for it disappears more quickly than we might wish.

Learning to read opens up a whole world of adventure created on the stage of the human mind. Friends occupy an increasingly prominent place as children mature. The early teen years often bring the warm glow of first romance, along with perplexing fluctuations in moods, hair styles, and fashions. Soon after that, many adolescents leave the family nest to establish an independent base of operations. For many, careers are launched, long-term commitments are made, and the cycle of life begins once again with a new generation.

Throughout the lifelong process of growth, our development is guided by two major factors—genetic predispositions, and opportunities to learn and to interact with the world around us. All human experience, from physical stature and appearance to personality and habitual response patterns, are steered by the detailed blueprints carried in our genes. Much of the consistency we observe in ourselves and others is rooted here. How else could we recognize the childhood photos of people we have known only as adults? In addition, however, stability and continuity come from the long-term relationships to which we commit ourselves and the cherished values we espouse. These go a long way in defining our individual identities that remain remarkably constant throughout our lives.

Ages and Stages of Development

Developmental psychologists start their study at the beginning, examining the miracles of conception and birth. Although you won't remember it, your life began as a single cell with a full complement of forty-six chromosomes, the carriers of your hereditary blueprint. During the next nine months, while your parents were preparing for your arrival, you developed at an explosive rate in the security of your mother's uterus. There you were equipped for the challenges and dangers of the hostile environment into which you were suddenly thrust at birth.

A newborn human, unlike most other infant creatures, is vulnerable to neglect or mistreatment and remains almost totally dependent on the loving care of others for several years. The most visible aspects of development that occur during the first few months are increasing motor capabilities and growing social attachments. The healthy infant steadily passes a series of developmental milestones obvious to every curious onlooker—rolling over, sitting up, standing more or less upright, and those first faltering steps. This sequence of achievements occurs at surprisingly predictable ages, with progress stemming largely from the infant's maturing nervous system. At the same time, the security of loving concern and abundant physical contact provide the foundation of trust on which social relationships can be built.

After the infant's first year, development appears to slow, but becomes increasingly diverse and multifaceted. Steady progress can be charted in a wide variety of dimensions at the same time—physical, emotional, mental, social, and moral to name a few. To facilitate understanding of the complexities of human growth, theorists have attempted to chart progress in physical, mental, or social dimensions in terms of series of developmental periods. As a result, much of our understanding of childhood growth is captured in the proposals of stage theorists such as Piaget, Erikson, and Kohlberg.

Jean Piaget was one of the most influential thinkers in all of psychology. His genius was to show that children think, not just less skillfully than adults, but in categorically different ways. On the basis of painstaking observations of children at various ages, Piaget proposed that mental development normally progresses through four major and distinct stages: *sensorimotor, pre-operational, concrete operational,* and *formal operational.* He contended that at each stage, the cognitive activities of children are marked by categorical differences in how they deal with the mental representations. This process culminates in the abstract thinking abilities of the final stage.

Erik Erikson's theory, comprising eight stages in all, addresses social and emotional development throughout the lifespan. At each stage, individuals face a unique crisis that may be resolved in either a healthy or a restricting fashion, depending on their experiences at that particular stage. For example, during the teen years, when the crisis is one of *identity vs. role-confusion*, adolescents need to establish a solid sense of who they are as individuals in order to continue developing in a healthy manner.

Lawrence Kohlberg's theory (which we will analyze shortly) is especially intriguing because it attempts to describe the course of moral development. He argues that moral maturity is achieved by moving through three levels of reasoning—preconventional, conventional, and postconventional. Kohlberg maintains that moral reasoning patterns are closely linked with behavior, but that most adults never achieve mature moral thinking.

Developmental psychologists have traditionally focused their study on the periods of most dramatic change, primarily early childhood and adolescence. In these early stages, there is a greater degree of predictability, for many unique traits have not yet had much opportunity to manifest themselves. However, in recent years, some of the attention previously directed to childhood and adolescence has been diverted to adulthood and old age. This shift is motivated in part by the social reality of an aging population. It also reflects an awareness that development never stops as long as we are living human beings.

Later in this chapter, we will explore implications of the final developmental stage—death—for those of us who grieve the loss of loved ones. But first, let us attempt to resolve the question of whether Kohlberg's theory of moral development makes sense within a Christian understanding of persons.

Development of Moral Reasoning: Is It Biblically Valid?

Kohlberg's understanding of moral development is tied to the goal of providing justice for an increasing number of people (1981). In this view, morally immature individuals are concerned only for themselves. As they progress, their choices reflect concern for friends and for the larger community as well. If moral growth proceeds to the highest levels, concern for justice extends to the entire human family.

In the levels of development that he identified, Kohlberg emphasized moral reasoning, a perspective that links morality with cognitive capacities. His method of investigation was most intriguing. Short stories known as *moral dilemmas* depicted a hypothetical character who was facing a difficult choice. People of various ages were confronted with these stories and were asked to indicate what course of action the story's central character should take. Even more significant, however, was the line of reasoning that these readers used in defending their choices.

A variety of moral dilemmas have been presented to hundreds of people since Kohlberg first proposed his stage theory. However, the seeds of his understanding were based on intensive investigation of a few dozen young male research subjects living in the Chicago area. From his analyses of their responses to his stories, Kohlberg proposed that people progress through some or all of six stages (he later added a seventh stage) of reasoning as they mature morally. We will focus only on the three broad levels (each comprising two substages) that Kohlberg initially identified. These are most often labeled the preconventional, the conventional, and the postconventional levels.

All children aged about nine or younger (along with many older children and some adults) can be classified at the *preconventional* level of moral reasoning. This stage is characterized by decision making based on expected consequences. A behavior such as stealing is judged as morally wrong if it is likely to be followed by punishment. Similarly, an activity like fighting might be judged right if the person gains rewards from it. At this level, the consequences are much more than an extra incentive to direct behavior. They provide the basis for judging whether something is morally right or wrong. Thus, a college student who has a chance to cheat on an assignment in a way that cannot be detected will freely do so if he is reasoning at Kohlberg's preconventional level.

After age nine, some but not nearly all children and teens progress to the *conventional* level. At this stage, the emphasis is on conformity—doing what is expected and accepted. A child who argues that bullying behavior is wrong because other people disapprove of it is displaying conventional-level reasoning.

Similarly, an action such as helping a lost child find her way home is good because this is the behavior expected in our society. A student who refrains from cheating because she knows about society's standards against it is making a typical conventional-level judgment of morality.

Those who can think in abstract terms (young teens and adults) become capable of Kohlberg's highest moral level, *post-conventional* reasoning. Although the majority of the population never reaches this stage, those who do so make their judgments based on abstract moral principles to which they have committed themselves. These principles might include justice for all, love for one's neighbor, or treating others the way one wishes to be treated. Students who reason at this level might decline the opportunity to cheat because such behavior would be inconsistent with their personal commitment to honesty.

Developmental-stage theories are intended to assist us in understanding typical changes that occur over time. Although this is the case with Kohlberg's theory, there is another value worth mentioning. To the extent that moral actions stem from more mature thinking, it seems a worthy goal to encourage the development of moral reasoning. Kohlberg argued that to stimulate moral growth, we need to help people identify their current moral level and then expose them to the thinking typical of the next higher stage. This has useful implications for Christian education, since right living is an important part of Christian maturity.

Although Kohlberg's work has been widely cited, not all reaction has been positive. One concern that frequently arises is the fact that moral reasoning is not the same as moral behavior. Clearly, one can understand higher levels of morality without acting accordingly. Research does suggest that people classified at Kohlberg's higher levels demonstrate higher ethical standards in their behavior, but the relationship is far from perfect. It could be argued that high levels of moral reasoning are necessary for consistent moral action, but that the motivation to behave morally is needed as well. Thus it must be kept in mind that preconventional, conventional, and postconventional levels describe progressions in moral understanding and not necessarily growth in practical morality.

A more fundamental concern arises when we attempt to apply these levels as a universal description of moral development. In her assessment of Kohlberg's work, Carol Gilligan (1982) points to the fact that the reasoning Kohlberg describes is more characteristic of men than women. Recall that Kohlberg's original group of subjects was an exclusively male sample, and that abstract moral dilemmas were used to explore reasoning patterns. Without attempting to divide moral reasoning neatly along gender lines, Gilligan makes a strong case that there are other appropriate ways of exploring moral decision making.

In her own studies involving female subjects, Gilligan interviewed women who had faced the real moral choice of aborting their own babies. She characterizes her conception of morality as an *ethic of caring* rather than a *logic of justice*. In her view, Kohlberg's system places undue emphasis on individual growth and decision making. For Gilligan, relationships and connectedness are at the heart of morality, a contrast with Kohlberg's emphasis on rights and rules.

The levels that Kohlberg identified are well worth considering, as are Gilligan's complementary proposals. Let us now consider how Christian perspectives help us come to terms with issues of moral development.

The Perspective of Faith

There can be no question that God cares about how we live—about our morality. (See, for example, Prov. 20:7; Matt. 19:20; 1 John 2:29.) The closely related themes of justice and righteousness are among the most prominent in all of Scripture. Thus Kohlberg can be affirmed in his attempt to deal with an important topic. His concern with moral development is one shared by the entire Christian church.

It is interesting to reflect on the way God has dealt with his people throughout history. Motet (1978) argues that initially God taught his people through consequences—miracles of deliverance and provision, and punishment for wrong actions. Later he provided the law, summarized in the Ten Commandments, and spelled out in a comprehensive system of rules that brought order to the nation. Much later, Christ came to change the hearts of his people and to teach the principle of love as the primary guideline for all relationships. These periods of history are remarkably parallel to Kohlberg's three stages.

In addition, Jesus' life and teachings can be understood in terms of Kohlberg's levels of moral development (Clouse 1985). Each stage both incorporates and extends the morality contained in the one it replaces. In a similar way, Jesus affirmed the law but also reinterpreted its meaning in terms of principles of right thought and attitude (Matt. 5:17–48). He modeled the principle of love to the point of self-sacrifice, particularly in his substitutionary death for us, and at times refused to be confined by either the law or the expectations of others (Matt. 12:8–12; Mark 2:23–27). As a model of perfect humanity, Jesus clearly demonstrated principled moral reasoning. Our lives should reflect his example.

However, Kohlberg's system of moral reasoning is not without its flaws. As already noted, his whole conception of morality is cognitive and abstract, far removed from practical living. Gilligan's use of real-life choices seems more appropriate than the mental gymnastics involved in solving hypothetical moral dilemmas. We need closer links between reasoning and life.

A second concern has to do with the self-oriented flavor of Kohlberg's stages. Although the highest level of reasoning reflects broad concerns with justice and the welfare of others, its emphasis is clearly on the individual's right to choose the principles to which commitments will be made. The parallel with the situation in ancient Israel, where "everyone did as he saw fit" (Judg. 21:25), is unmistakable. Kohlberg offers no basis for deciding which principles are worthy of choice. Thus his entire conception of morality is devoid of content.

Finally, while the concern with encouraging progress in moral development is commendable, we cannot assume that exposure to the reasoning of the next higher stage will necessarily result in growth. We humans have an addiction to sin. Morality as it is understood in Scripture is based primarily on a change of heart and on worthy models. Parents and leaders are exhorted to set appropriate examples for others to follow (Prov. 22:6; Tit. 2:7–8). In Kohlberg's scheme, the role of heroes is missing. However, the motivation behind costly deeds of courage and moral integrity probably derives more from challenging examples than from abstract reasoning.

A Limited Endorsement

The ability of stage theories to capture morality and its development will continue to be debated for some time. Nevertheless, Kohlberg's views on moral reasoning have made a useful contribution to our understanding.

Two points merit particular emphasis. First, we should note that morality is a complex topic. Kohlberg's theory focuses on the cognitive dimensions of moral development, aspects that are important although not comprehensive. One's actions will not likely be guided by moral principles unless one can reason at the higher levels. Second, general principles of behavior are compatible with Christian perspectives, provided these principles are biblically valid. We ought to behave morally, not for the reward gained or for the approval of others, but because we have committed ourselves to what we know to be right.

One final observation concerns the notion of tolerance and respect for others. Although Jesus did not condone sin in any form, particularly in those who knew better, he did display a profound respect for other people, regardless of their behavior or values. This valuing of the person can sometimes be neglected, as in our fervent commitment to the letter of the law. For this reason, Kohlberg's contention that we need to be guided by appropriate moral principles is a timely reminder for Christians.

Good Grief

Even though death is probably the most certain aspect of human experience, most of us display great ingenuity in avoiding the subject. We are a death-denying culture, much more comfortable with an emphasis on youth and health. Despite the recent research focus on death and dying stemming from the insightful work of Elisabeth Kübler-Ross (1969) with terminally ill persons, most of us still seek to avoid the reality of death. There is great value, however, in understanding the grieving process. This will prepare us to cope more adequately with our own experiences of grief when they come. As well, we will be better equipped to provide support for friends who are grieving.

Bereavement refers to the loss of someone close, a person whose life was intertwined with ours. The normal result of bereavement is mourning or grief—the intense and painful jungle of emotions through which we must try to find our way. Grief has been described as "the other side of the coin of love" (Jackson 1980, 88). Throughout our lives, we form bonds of attachment with people around us. It is through these bonds that we derive meaning, pleasure, and satisfaction in life. These bonds take time to establish, and when they must be broken, the process is a painful one. The stronger the bond and the greater the love shared between people, the more intense will be the pain of separation. We do not grieve for those we have not loved.

Each person's experience of grieving will in some ways be unique, for our personalities, cultural backgrounds, and relationships vary widely. Nevertheless, several manifestations of grief are typical. It is helpful to know what to expect.

When the news of a friend's or a family member's death first comes, almost everyone experiences shock. This involves a sense of unreality and a vague hope that one will awaken to find that it was all a bad dream. In addition, guilt is normal, since none of us have done all we could for others, and we must face the fact that such opportunities are gone forever. We often feel angry as well, and may direct that anger toward medical personnel, family members, or even God. Usually a grieving person feels an overwhelming sense of isolation and loneliness, a feeling of being completely alone in his suffering. As well, grief typically brings a disturbing array of physical symptoms—uncontrollable crying, sleeplessness and fatigue, intense anxiety, and inability to focus or concentrate. All of these are normal, although they ordinarily subside within a few weeks.

Because the experience of grieving is painful, our natural inclination is to brush aside the feelings of hurt and loneliness. Yet the resolution and healing that eventually comes is contingent on our walking through the pain. It is important to experience the painful feelings rather than to deny them. As Kouri has wisely said, "Grief is patient; whatever you leave undone just sits there waiting for you" (1991, 39). This is why we often need the support of family and friends. When the waves of painful emotions and memories roll in, we may be overwhelmed and unable to face them unless someone who cares is sitting with us in our grief.

In his sensitive discussion of the process of mourning at various stages in the life cycle, Crenshaw (1990) proposes that grieving involves emotional and psychological work. Several tasks make up the work of grieving. The completion of each one contributes to a healthy resolution to the grieving process. First we must face the reality and finality of death. Also, we need to express our grief and rediscover that we can trust other people to care and love us. The next task is to honor the loved one who has died, perhaps by picking up a commitment that this person was unable to complete. Probably the most difficult task—the one in which the grieving process is most often stalled—is acknowledging the mixture of positive and negative feelings we have toward the deceased individual and arriving at an honest balance in these feelings. This will be particularly difficult when our relationship was an unhappy and painful one. The final tasks involve letting go emotionally, releasing the loved one who has died, and reinvesting feelings in other appropriate relationships. This makes it possible for grieving persons to move ahead by restructuring their plans and activities in light of the fact that the loved one is no longer a part of their lives.

Grief is good. It should not be thought of as a nuisance or an enemy, for in walking through our pain, we emerge with a deep inner strength. Crenshaw suggests that "recovery from grief means you can face and bear the loss, but you are permanently changed as a result of the experience" (1990, 28). The goal of the process is not to forget your loved one; it is rather to reach closure so you can remember that person without the intense pain and with a measure of contentment.

How can we reach out to those who mourn? If we are to help others, we must accept the fact that we cannot and should not spare them the pain of mourning. What we can do is be a companion in their grief. The following suggestions are offered to those who genuinely care and wish to help.

1. Resist the tendency to talk too much. Your main task is to listen or to sit in silence and hurt with your friend. Your presence says much more than your words.

2. Don't say "I know how you feel," because you don't. You might say "I am hurting with you" or "You must be feeling deep pain." This gives your friend permission to verbalize feelings.

3. Refer to the person who has died by name; describe something about that person that has special meaning for you.

4. Try to make the grieving person feel accepted in the confusion of feelings. Encourage the expression of grief in words, by crying, or in overt actions.

5. Resist the urge to pull the grieving person out of his grief with comments like "Your mother is better off now" or "It's not so bad." This may be true, but it is not helpful.

6. Refer again to the deceased friend or relative several weeks or months later, and ask your friend how she is feeling. She has not forgotten, and may need to verbalize her feelings repeatedly to work through them.

7. Especially in the early stages, provide practical assistance by chauffeuring children, bringing in meals, or cutting the lawn.

8. Encourage the bereaved individual to honor the loved one in a practical way—visiting the grave, planting a tree in memory, writing a poem or a letter, or joining a cause that mattered to the loved one.

9. Be patient. Give time and room for the tasks of mourning to be accomplished.

10. If you sense that your friend is not coping with the pain, gently encourage the person to seek help through a grief counselor or a group of fellow mourners.

Our compassionate God thoroughly understands and deeply hurts when we grieve. The Bible indicates this in various words—"precious in the sight of the LORD is the death of his saints" (Ps. 116:15) and "the LORD is close to the brokenhearted" (Ps. 34:18). Furthermore, we are instructed to "mourn with those who mourn" (Rom. 12:15) and to "carry each other's burdens" (Gal. 6:2). There are few more effective ways we can minister to others than by accompanying them in their grief so that they can bear the pain and not lose hope. In working through it to a positive resolution, they will indeed be able to experience the priceless benefits of *good grief.*

Cognitive Development and Spiritual Growth

Throughout its history, the Christian church has struggled to reconcile faith with reason. Some maintain that the two are in opposition, with human logic posing a threat to true faith, while others see faith carrying on when reason has reached its limit. Therefore, it is useful to explore the relevance of individual cognitive development for spiritual growth.

The best known attempt to do this is found in James Fowler's stages of faith (1986). He proposes seven types or levels of faith arranged in ascending order of maturity, roughly correlated with a person's age. Fowler's work depends heavily on Piaget, and his stage theory has been criticized as overly cognitive in its emphasis. In addition, faith is generic, or as he defines it, "a way of leaning into life" (Fowler 1986, 16). As such, it is more closely related to meaning and purpose in life than to faith in the uniquely Christian sense. While Fowler's insights have value, clearly faith in a personal God is more than this.

In her recent article on faith and cognitive development, Krych (1992) argues that we must be careful to avoid both of two attractive extremes. Faith and cognitive growth should not be too closely linked, but neither should we ignore their relationship. Certainly, our patterns of spiritual growth interact with development in all dimensions, cognitive ones included. A child's concept of God will change as he matures mentally; his understanding of the biblical account of human experience will not remain constant. It is clear, however, that saving faith is a gift from God (Eph. 2:8) that does not rest on human understanding alone. Faith involves a commitment to Christ and a growing relationship with him, aspects that clearly go beyond the cognitive domain. The biblical injunction to "become as little children" (Matt. 18:3) suggests that faith is not closely tied to cognitive capacity.

Provided we realize that faith is related to but not synonymous with cognition, we can derive several valuable insights from a grasp of cognitive developmental patterns. First, while the faith of a child or mentally challenged person is genuine, it is different from the faith of an adult. A child's concept of who God is will evolve as the child matures cognitively and otherwise. Secondly, our efforts to teach biblical truths and principles need to take cognitive level into account. Young children are prone to distortions and partial understanding, as illustrated by the boy who reported having learned at church about "Gladly, the cross-eyed bear." We need to communicate directly and concretely, emphasizing stories from the life of Jesus and other Bible characters, as well as foundational truths such as the love of God. Finer points of doctrine can come later.

By contrast, since adults have the capacity for abstract thought, it is appropriate to challenge them with meaty theological concepts from the writings of Paul, Peter, and others. Finally, we should recognize that certain developmental stages, most notably adolescence, offer the greatest readiness for Christian conversion. A corresponding emphasis on faith commitments is particularly appropriate at this stage. Not only are teenagers capable of understanding abstract truth, but also they are searching for a sense of their own identity and for meaning in life. Commitment to Christ facilitates their development on both counts.

Effective planting for a harvest of faith is made possible as we gain clearer understanding of those to whom we seek to communicate. The developmental stage theories of Piaget and others are useful in this regard.

Reflecting Back

In this chapter, the emphasis has been on **growth**, for the developmental process begins at conception and continues throughout life. Growth is frequently described in terms of discrete stages representing progress in mental, social, or moral domains. However, these distinct steps should not blind us to the essential continuity of lifelong human development.

In exploring moral development, we discovered that Kohlberg's stages help bring into focus our need to commit ourselves to biblical principles of conduct rather than to follow a set of rules. However, we also noted that this theory is heavily cognitive and omits the important elements of relationships and modeling.

In exploring the natural human process of grieving and in reflecting on how faith grows, we noted a variety of insights that psychology provides. Through understanding and applying them, we can better serve those who mourn and can effectively teach the truths of the Christian faith to people of all ages.

Going Deeper

1. For some valuable reflections on how Kohlberg's theory of moral development relates to Scripture, read "Moral reasoning and Christian faith" by Bonnidell Clouse, *Journal of Psychology and Theology* 13 (1985): 190–98.
2. For an excellent discussion of the process of grieving at different stages in the life cycle, I warmly recommend David Crenshaw's *Bereavement* (Continuum, 1990).
3. For a personal view of the intense pain of losing a child, you might ponder Nicholas Wolterstorff's *Lament for a Son* (Eerdmans, 1987).
4. For a concise treatment of the relationship between mental and spiritual growth, see "Faith and cognitive development" by Margaret Krych, in *Christian Perspectives on Human Development*, edited by L. Aden, D. Benner, and J. H. Ellens (Baker, 1992).

9

Human Personality

As a young adult, I encountered Tim LaHaye's description of four basic personality types or temperaments and was intrigued. He defined the temperaments by their corresponding lists of strengths and weaknesses, and illustrated each with a prominent biblical character (LaHaye 1966). I can easily remember them yet. Moses the *melancholic* was inventor of a thousand excuses when God called him, but also showed unparalleled devotion and self-sacrifice. Peter the *sanguine* loved to be in the middle of the action. He often spoke first and thought later, but his heart was right. Abraham the *phlegmatic* needed a push to get started, but showed remarkable composure and skill in the crunch and was steady as a rock. The apostle Paul was a typical *choleric*, so goal-oriented that he sometimes trampled on others in the process, but a man of tremendous drive and accomplishment.

The temperaments were easy for me to understand, even if their names were a little strange. Besides, they highlighted a significant fact: People are different. They helped me understand my brother's unwavering focus on finishing a project, my mother's apparently infinite patience, and my wife's love of being with people. These differing characteristics reflect the unique personality of each individual.

Seeing the Bigger Picture

When students enroll in a first course in psychology, they usually bring lofty expectations of gaining more freedom from their parents, understanding why their friends are so moody, and capturing the perfect date. Studies of neurotransmitters, operant conditioning, and Piaget's stages are therefore more than a little disappointing! In applying a scientific grid to the study of human experience, the living breathing person seems to get buried.

It is the study of personality that provides this bigger picture. So far, we have examined selected aspects of our experiences— taking in sensory information, forgetting yesterday's lecture, and being driven to achieve our goals. But in their study of personality, prominent theorists such as Sigmund Freud, Carl Jung, and Abraham Maslow attempted to explain how these pieces fit together to create each unique individual.

Personality theorists are less concerned about scientific rigor and experimental control. Much of their work involves theorizing, speculating, and attempting to construct creative models of what makes people tick. They each sketch an understanding that is unique; however, all of them deal in some way with core issues of personality function. They must explain the structure or the component parts of the personality. As well, they need to account for personality dynamics—how these parts work together to motivate specific behaviors. Finally, all theorists must deal with development, the way in which the uniqueness of each individual comes about.

In some ways, all of psychology is the study of personality, for there is no aspect of our experience that personality theorists are willing to ignore. However, the unique contribution of these specialists is the attempt to fit the pieces together into a coherent account of why we learn and remember and forget and develop and get depressed and relate with others as we do. They are also interested in ways that each person is an individual.

The Range of Views on Personality

To study personality, it is useful to measure how much of various traits each person displays. Personality assessment is often done by questionnaires in which you describe yourself by responding *agree* or *disagree* to statements such as "When I feel bored, I like to stir up trouble." More creative assessment tools involve showing people pictures and asking them to make up stories about them, or having people complete open-ended sentences such as "Being successful in your work is. . . ." One unusual test is called the Rorschach. It has people describe what they see in a series of meaningless designs created by spilling ink on paper and folding the paper over to make a symmetrical pattern. The assumption is that what people see in these ambiguous patterns will reveal something about their inner feelings and motives.

The four temperaments we met earlier comprise the simplest kind of trait theory. According to this view, everyone can be classified into a dominant personality type or cluster of characteristics. More frequently, however, trait theorists identify dimensions that they believe account for the most important differences between people. These major scales usually include introversion-extroversion, level of anxiety, and emotionality-rationality. The idea is that each person displays a unique and enduring cluster of traits, and that this consistent pattern defines the personality.

Other personality theories are not concerned about measuring traits at all. The humanistic approach focuses on the *self*, which is seen as the core of human personality. Critical to effective personal adjustment and functioning is a healthy view of ourselves. According to Carl Rogers and other self-theorists, we need a climate of acceptance and esteem in which to realize our full potential as persons.

Freud's widely publicized psychoanalytic theory proposes that three key elements make up the personality: the id, the ego, and the superego. The *id* represents basic inherited drives that push for expression. The *superego* functions like a conscience, formed out of the expectations of others, which we have internalized. The *ego* seeks to maintain balance between the other two elements and to stay in touch with reality. As illustrated in Freud's iceberg analogy, much of the personality functions below the level of conscious awareness. Because personality development occurs mostly during childhood, early experiences and relationships are of particular importance.

Several of Freud's disciples developed modified versions of psychoanalytic theory. Jung expanded the concept of the unconscious to emphasize the importance of a society's *collective unconscious* revealed in its myths and symbols. Alfred Adler agreed with the special importance of childhood experiences, but felt that the struggle to overcome feelings of inferiority was most critical for personality development.

Behavioral and cognitive approaches to personality build on research in their respective areas. Behaviorists emphasize observable actions as they are shaped by the physical and social environment. Their view of personality suggests that people are less a product of enduring traits or self-concepts and more defined by the activities in which they engage. The consistency we observe in people (extroverts, for example) stems mainly from their tendency to seek rewarding situations with plenty of other people and lots of exciting activities. According to cognitive theorists, our interpretations of the situations we find ourselves in help to define our personality and to determine our responses.

Having briefly surveyed the most prominent personality theories, we turn next to the important topic of self-esteem. Our purpose is to discover how it relates to the concepts of pride, humility, and Christian commitment.

Is High Self-Esteem Good or Bad?

Do you ever talk to yourself? Most of us engage often in imaginary conversations in which we say, "It sure feels good to get that exam over," or "I wonder why I'm so depressed today," or "I did a really good job defusing that argument." Our self-talk often has an evaluative dimension as we pass judgment on our own activities and capabilities.

The distinctively human capacity for self-consciousness makes it possible for us to monitor not only others' but also our own behaviors, thoughts, and motives. *Self-esteem* represents the degree of positiveness or negativeness in these ongoing self-assessments. It is a concept that most psychologists consider to be of fundamental importance. Level of self-esteem has been found to correlate with such characteristics as ability to cope with stress, response to others' criticism, ability to form satisfying interpersonal relationships, and capacity to resist persuasive influences (Brockner 1988). Clearly, it is an important aspect of personality.

Self-esteem is presumably a universal human characteristic. Obviously, its level varies from person to person, as does the strength of other personality traits. It has been suggested that self-esteem comprises two facets: a sense of personal worth and a sense of efficacy or capacity for effective action (Aycock and Noaker 1985). The concept of self-esteem is particularly crucial in western society, with its heavy emphasis on individual accomplishment.

The level of self-esteem is usually assessed by means of a personality questionnaire in which people rate the accuracy of a series of self-descriptive statements. According to Stanley Coopersmith (1967), who carefully explored how one's self-concept develops, it is formed primarily through the comments and judgments made by parents and significant others whose affirmation we seek. Self-esteem appears to fluctuate somewhat from moment to moment based on moods and experiences of success or failure. Presumably, it rises after you take an easy test and plunges temporarily after an especially tough one. Generally, however, it appears to remain relatively stable over the lifespan, once it has been established.

Among clinicians and counselors, there is wide recognition of the impact of self-esteem on psychological adjustment. They find that mental and emotional problems are often associated with poor self-image. Depressed people in particular may suffer from a painfully low sense of worth, and counselors may seek to strengthen a client's shaky self-esteem. People judged most successful in relationships and in life as a whole manifest much more positive self-assessment. For these reasons, healthy self-esteem is highly valued.

The Perspective of Faith

Due to the popularity of humanistic perspectives on personality, the "self" and "self-esteem" became household words. Christians have responded to these developments with a mixture of support, concern, and confusion. Robert Schuller (1982) is convinced that a solid sense of worth is every person's most basic need and is God's intention for each of us who bear his image. The church must address that need or become obsolete. He believes that the biblical message provides the answer to the universal human longing for a sense of worth, but that the message must be focused on that need so that people will be drawn to Christ.

In *The Biblical View of Self-Esteem, Self-Love and Self-Image*, Jay Adams takes a very different position. He argues that the emphasis on the self is misplaced and contrary to the biblical message. Efforts to justify the legitimacy of self-esteem come at the expense of distorting and twisting the truth of Scripture. According to Adams, the Bible's primary message is a call for self-denial rather than self-esteem (Matt. 16:24–25). On this issue, he maintains that psychological views and scriptural teaching represent "two utterly diverse and irreconcilable paths" (1986, 105).

A further concern with the concept of self-esteem in the light of biblical truth centers on the sin of pride. Arrogance and pride are condemned in Scripture (Prov. 8:13; James 4:6) as something God hates. We are warned as well that pride leads to personal disaster (Prov. 16:18). In addition, a spirit of humility is consistently affirmed (Prov. 15:33; Luke 14:10; Gal. 6:14), with Jesus' self-sacrificing death on our behalf representing the supreme example. If a positive self-concept is linked with pride and incompatible with humility, it clearly has no place in the life of a disciple of Christ.

Surrounding this topic is not only disagreement but a good deal of confusion and misunderstanding as well. Let us attempt to clarify the meaning of these concepts and to discover whether a reconciliation between relevant psychological and biblical insights can be achieved.

Toward a Clearer Understanding

Throughout Scripture, the human trait of love for oneself is recognized and assumed, though never commanded (1 Sam. 20:17; Matt. 22:39). This is not a license for excessive and narcissistic self-love (2 Tim. 3:2), but an indication of the type and extent of concern for others we should display. Thus reasonable self-love is a natural, normal, and perhaps even necessary characteristic (Eph. 5:28–29).

Elsewhere in Scripture, we are instructed not to evaluate ourselves more highly than is reasonable and appropriate (Rom. 12:3), and to regard the concerns of others as having equal or higher priority than our own (Phil. 2:3–4). Coupling this teaching with Jesus' appeal to each of his disciples to "deny himself and take up his cross" (Luke 9:23), it is possible to conclude that a healthy sense of self-worth is inappropriate for the follower of Christ.

The notion that humans have inherent value makes some Christians uncomfortable because they interpret this affirmation of worth as a denial of our fallen, sinful nature. The doctrine of *total depravity* is at times thought to mean that ever since the fall of our species through Adam's sin, there has remained nothing of value in humankind. However, a critical distinction needs to be made at this point between two related but different concepts—worthy and worthful. David Clark (1985) suggests that according to Scripture, humans are clearly *unworthy* of God's mercy and favor, but without question are of tremendous value and are *full of worth* in God's eyes. Worthy or deserving we are not; of great worth and value we certainly are.

The reason for this worth lies in our having been created in God's majestic image, an image tarnished and distorted by the fall, but not entirely obliterated in even the worst of us. Adolf Hitler still differed from an animal or a devil and reflected at least a glimmer of the original image of the Creator. Likewise, each of us has worth. The evidence that God sees all of us, including people you or I might judge as despicable, as having great worth is twofold. He places far more value on us than on the rest of his creation (Matt. 6:26). In addition, he chose to redeem us at infinite cost—the very life of his Son.

We conclude that every individual is a person of worth. Thus, a healthy, realistic appreciation of one's own value is not displeasing to God. The issue we must yet resolve is how pride and humility relate to self-esteem. Schuller (1982) makes a helpful distinction between positive and negative pride. Destructive arrogance or *negative pride* is an attitude of superiority over others and independence from God, and God hates it. The essence of *positive pride* is confidence and contentment, a sense of gratitude and accomplishment in the productive use of our gifts. It is not based on comparison with others, but is rooted instead in a realistic sense of our own importance and our complete dependence on God (Gal. 6:3–4).

Perhaps you have observed people belittling themselves. "What humble people!" you may have thought. Nothing could be further from the truth. People with a low sense of self-worth subtly but effectively draw attention to themselves in an effort to bolster their self-assessment. In essence, both arrogance and self-hate are the same. The person who regularly depreciates himself is in bondage to himself. And someone once observed, "A person wrapped up in himself makes a very small package."

What then is true humility? It is being so absorbed with the welfare of others that one has little time left over to think about oneself. I know a person like that. When he talks to someone, either close friend or complete stranger, he devotes his full attention to that individual. In so doing, he communicates a profound sense of respect for that person. He regularly leaves those he encounters feeling affirmed, fully alive, and uplifted in spirit. If you were to ask him about his self-esteem, he would be puzzled, for he wastes little time focusing on himself. Clark captures the idea succinctly: "True humility is neither thinking too much of oneself, nor too little of oneself; it is not thinking of oneself at all" (1985, 9). It is the combination of healthy self-respect and true humility—a gift of grace—that enables us to invest our lives in serving others, following the pattern set by Jesus himself.

Having focused on one important dimension of personality, we step back now to look again at the bigger picture. Although the Bible does not present a systematic theory of personality, it has valuable insight to offer on the meaning of personhood.

A Biblical View of the Person

It is characteristic of secular psychology to seek explanations of human experience apart from God. Van Leeuwen observes that "most personality theories are expressing truths about human nature, albeit in misguided form" (1985, 230). Thus we need a biblical perspective in order to correctly understand the insights contained in these theories. The truths about human nature found in Scripture focus largely on our relationship with God and our need for the salvation he alone can provide. Nevertheless, we can use them as a foundation and a framework for a genuinely Christian understanding of persons.

Clues to the nature of human personality are found in the words used in Scripture to describe people and the various components that make up the person. McDonald (1986) identifies four significant terms and discusses their use in Scripture. These terms are *flesh*, *body*, *soul*, and *spirit*.

When the term *flesh* is used in the Bible, it usually refers to fallen human nature. This is the meaning in Galatians 5:16, where Paul asserts, "live by the Spirit and you will not gratify the desires of the sinful nature" (i.e., the flesh). A similar reference to "putting off the sinful nature" occurs in Colossians 2:11. The closest psychological parallel to the flesh is probably Freud's concept of the *id*, which represents our storehouse of selfish and pleasure-seeking drives.

The term *body* used in Scripture refers to the physical, material aspect of our humanness. Contrary to the Greek understanding in which the body is devalued and seen as the main source of evil, the biblical notion is that the body is to be given to God (Rom. 12:1) and is to be God's dwelling place (1 Cor. 6:19–20). More importantly, our bodies will one day be resurrected (1 Cor. 15:42–44; Phil. 3:21). Clearly, the brain, the inner organs, and the senses that psychologists study are all parts of the body which Christ wishes to inhabit and which he will one day fully restore.

Of special interest in psychology is the term *soul* or *psyche*, from which the word *psychology* derives. Its most typical meaning is living being or person (Lev. 7:21; Rom. 2:9), but it is translated in a wide variety of ways including heart, self, and mind. It does not usually refer to the immaterial part of humans, although this is an application we often make when we speak of the body and soul being separated at death.

The final term is *spirit*, which literally means breath. In its most common biblical usage, it is understood as the principle of life, and it often points to our capacity to relate to God. The spiritual person (Gal. 6:1) is someone who knows God through direct personal experience.

We might wish to match up biblical and psychological terms neatly, but the words in Scripture referring to various aspects of our humanness do not have a consistent and predictable usage. Some scholars have tried to defend a three-part view of personality based on verses such as 1 Thessalonians 5:23, which includes reference to the terms *body, soul,* and *spirit.* This is not justifiable, however, for the Bible does not treat these words as scientific terms. *Soul* is just as often used to refer to the whole person as to one (psychological) aspect of the individual. The most reasonable conclusion we can draw is that while there are different aspects to our humanity, each person is most fundamentally a *unity,* a whole being. Just as God is one, so are we.

Granting that a neat compartmentalization of dimensions of the personality is not possible, what significant characteristics does the Bible attribute to humankind? First and most fundamental is our personhood. We are not mere victims of our own inner impulses, nor are we passive responders to our environment. As persons, we take initiative, we make choices, and we are accountable to our Creator. Along with personhood, several other characteristics can be identified. We have dignity as God's image-bearers. We exist in relationship to God, to one another, and to his creation. Finally, we have the capacity to reflect on and evaluate our own activities—we are morally responsible—but we manifest a strong inclination to refuse God's rightful authority over us.

Personality theorists attempt to describe the dynamics of human nature—how the various facets of personhood fit together. VanLeeuwen (1985) reviews several models and concludes that a conflict model fits the biblical perspective best. At the core of our being we find two opposing tendencies. We are created for the security of a commitment to our Father; at the same time we are stubbornly inclined to pursue our own willful independence, even though it means sacrificing this highly prized security. In addition, however, the balance is decidedly tipped toward independence. The Bible makes it clear that in our unregenerate condition, we are not capable of seeking after God (Rom. 3:10–11). Only by his initiative and grace are we able to make a commitment to him.

The dual nature of humankind is clear in Scripture. According to Genesis 2:7, "The LORD God formed the man from the dust of the ground, and breathed into his nostrils the breath of life, and the man became a living being." In McDonald's words, "man is at once of nature and of God, a combination of dust and deity" (1986, 120). We are in some respects like God, for we bear his image. In other ways, however, our creaturely status is painfully obvious, for we are utterly dependent on him, and his image in us is badly tarnished.

Despite our dual nature, different aspects of which are emphasized by various personality theorists, we are one—a mind-body unity. We function as whole persons. We work, play, and relate with others emotionally, spiritually, mentally, and physically; these aspects cannot be separated. We are called to worship and love God with all of our minds, our hearts, our souls, and our strength—with our entire being (Mark 12:29).

Armed with this understanding of the broad outline of human personality found in Scripture, let us now examine more closely one fascinating component. Although many have tried to ignore the unconscious mind, it refuses to go away.

Is the Unconscious Mind Real?

Do you have an unconscious mind? Are there thoughts and feelings of which you have no awareness but that still influence your behavior in important ways? Most of us from time to time find ourselves doing something without knowing why. Apparently Paul had similar experiences, which he described vividly in Romans 7:15–20. More specific evidence for the presence of an unconscious mind comes from dreams and from slips of speech or writing. The content of our dreams often goes well beyond any conscious thoughts we have ever had, perhaps stemming from unconscious impulses. A good example of a slip of writing occurred when an outspoken critic of Sigmund Freud mistakenly spelled his name *Fraud*!

Prior to the advent of psychoanalytic theory, people preferred to think of themselves as rational creatures, doing what they did for good reasons and with full awareness. Freud went out on a long limb in taking exception to the prevailing view. He asserted that compared with conscious thoughts and motives, the irrational unconscious mind has a much more powerful influence on behavior. He characterized the unconscious mind as a bubbling cauldron of memories and impulses that are too threatening to admit to awareness. These feelings are therefore repressed or pushed down into the unconscious.

Although other psychologists have generally been skeptical of the unconscious, Freud and his followers developed the idea with considerable care. Evidence of the power of the unconscious to affect our behavior is found in cases of hysteria (e.g., sudden blindness with no organic cause), bizarre dreams, irrational habits, and slips of speech that reveal our true feelings. This mysterious and potentially painful domain can best be explored and brought to awareness with the help of a therapist using free association and dream analysis.

Objections to the reality of the unconscious mind have arisen from various sources. Behaviorists categorically deny the unconscious, finding no value in capacities we cannot directly observe. Humanists emphasize thoughts and feelings of which we are fully aware, for it is these that form the basis for our choices and goals. Brain researchers have tended to minimize the importance of the unconscious as well. Some have attempted to reduce this notion to hemispheric separation, citing as their evidence *split brain* studies (described in chapter 2). According to this view, information processed in the right hemisphere only may never reach full awareness.

For the most part, Christians have been skeptical of the unconscious as well, though for somewhat different reasons. They argue that it is implausible to suggest that God has an unconscious mind. Since we are created in his image, we probably don't have one either. In addition, because the unconscious is beyond our awareness, there is little we can do about it. Christians have been reluctant to consider a concept which suggests that we are not completely responsible for our actions.

Despite all these objections, the notion of an unconscious mind merits a second look. Without doubt, our rational nature is affirmed in a variety of Scripture passages (Isa. 1:18; 1 Cor. 14:15; 1 Pet. 3:15). The Bible also makes reference to puzzling aspects of the human personality that defy human comprehension, even though all our thoughts and motives are completely understood by God (Heb. 4:12–13). We have already alluded to Paul's struggles with frustrating and confusing urges that he describes in Romans 7. The psalmist requests that God search his heart and mind, apparently concerned that something he does not quite understand needs attention (Ps. 139:23–24). Likewise, the prophet Jeremiah's characterization of the human heart as "deceitful above all things," is followed by his rhetorical question, "Who can know it?" (Jer. 17:9). This suggests that there is much we do not understand about ourselves.

While the unconscious mind is somewhat mysterious and difficult to describe, there seems to be no biblical reason to deny its existence. Concerns to defend the idea of human responsibility are appropriate, but there may be no necessary conflict between a proper understanding of the unconscious and this important concept. For example, suppose that my unconscious mind is filled with repressed feelings of hatred or resentment because of my unwillingness to forgive someone who has harmed me. In this example, the influence of my unconscious malice originates in my refusal to obey the biblical injunction to forgive others. Thus I am still responsible, even though the root of my ill will is an unconscious one.

Besides the evidence found in dreams, slips of speech, and confusion about our own motives, the unconscious mind is implicated in a practice called the *healing of memories*. It has been the experience of Christian counselors such as David Seamands (1985) that believers are sometimes unable to move beyond their troubled past until painful memories have been dealt with. This process is one in which, bathed in prayer, the troubled person is guided by the Holy Spirit to focus on harmful memories that are long forgotten and to forgive those who have caused the hurt. While caution is advised, it is reasonable to expect that God, who understands completely both our conscious and our unconscious minds, is able to restore and to heal when we turn to him.

In conclusion, we have seen that while the unconscious mind is a somewhat speculative concept, there is considerable evidence from both psychology and Scripture to confirm its validity. After reviewing a wide range of evidence, William Kelly concludes that "there exists a dynamic unconscious that must be respected and dealt with in every major phase of life" (1991, 206). With additional effort by thoughtful Christians, a clearer and more biblically responsible understanding of the unconscious mind will be developed.

Reflecting Back

In our considerations throughout this chapter, we have been focusing on the **person**. Personality theories attempt to explain how the different dimensions of our human nature fit together, enabling us to function effectively. Each theory captures pieces of the picture, but each contains distortions as well. In some, the person is almost completely lost.

In psychology, healthy levels of self-esteem have repeatedly been shown to contribute to mature and productive human interactions. We attempted to better understand the biblical emphasis on self-denial and humility by noting that both pride and self-critical attitudes are usually linked to an inadequate sense of self-worth. A realistic and healthy self-image makes true humility and service to others possible.

Although the Bible deals primarily with our need for God rather than the structure of personality, it provides a firm foundation for a balanced understanding of the person. We have a dual nature, but the central emphasis of Scripture is on unity. Finally, we explored the possibility of a Christian understanding of the unconscious mind, concluding that this is an area ripe for further study.

Going Deeper

1. For a concise discussion of the question of human worth, I recommend "Philosophical reflections on self-worth and self-love" by David Clark, *Journal of Psychology and Theology* 13 (1985): 3–11.
2. For an analysis of biblical passages relating to the self, read Jay Adams's *The Biblical View of Self-Esteem, Self-Love, and Self-Image* (Harvest House, 1986).
3. For a good discussion of biblical terms that relate to the personality, see chapter 6 of Stan Jones's *Psychology and the Christian Faith* (Baker, 1986).

4. For a perceptive evaluation of various personality theories, consult chapter 10 in Mary Van Leeuwen's *The Person in Psychology* (Eerdmans, 1985).
5. For an overview of the place of the unconscious in psychological thinking, read William Kelly's *Psychology of the Unconscious* (Prometheus, 1991).

10

Normality and Pathology

The fourth chapter of the Book of Daniel in the Old Testament contains the almost unbelievable account of King Nebuchadnezzar's descent from luxurious self-indulgence into crippling madness. This dramatic change apparently occurred as a judgment from God for the king's foolish pride. For an extended period of time (probably several months), Nebuchadnezzar lived like an animal, growing long hair and claws and eating grass. Functionally, the king had become a wild beast. When he recognized who God really was, both his sanity and his position of power and prestige were dramatically restored.

An equally fascinating story unfolded while David was a fugitive from King Saul. As recorded in 1 Samuel 21:10–15, David feigned insanity in the presence of his captors in order to avoid reprisals from Achish, king of Gath. Fortunately for David, the ruse—one still used today—was effective and he was released unharmed. It is obvious from the account that King Achish was already familiar with madmen.

Does Anyone Know What Normal Means?

When psychologists attempt to define abnormal behavior, they face a formidable challenge. Obviously, abnormal means deviating from the norm or average. But how can we determine the norm? What exactly do we mean by normal behavior?

We can specify what normal means either by describing what *is* or by identifying what *ought to be*. The former involves a statistical definition in which behaviors occurring commonly are judged normal. On this basis, if nearly everyone was addicted to alcohol, then alcoholism would represent normal behavior. By contrast, those who displayed unusual generosity in their support for the cancer society would be viewed as abnormal. Because of the obvious inadequacy of this perspective, its supporters often introduce an additional criterion: Abnormal behavior is not only rare but socially unacceptable as well.

The second way of understanding normality uses an ethical or a moral definition. From this perspective, there is a standard of appropriate behavior, an objective criterion upon which actions may be judged as normal or abnormal, regardless of their popularity. This standard might be one given by God. However, if God is not part of the picture, it is difficult to agree on the standard. Thus, the definition of normal behavior preferred by psychologists is couched in terms of what is commonly practiced and thought of as acceptable by most people. Changes in normality in this sense can be expected to occur from time to time. A recent example is the dropping of homosexuality from the official list of abnormal behaviors.

For those who accept the Bible as God's special revelation to humans, the clearest definition of normality is found in the example of Jesus Christ. His life represented perfect humanity and complete normality. Clearly, he placed priority on service to others, he showed love to those who mistreated him, and he was calm and composed under stresses of the most extreme sort. Yet he was frequently misunderstood and criticized, even by those closest to him, and was occasionally accused of being mad.

Followers of Christ in this generation must work out corporately what it means for us to be normal. However, the norms of society are of little help, for in one sense, our whole culture is alienated from God and is not living normally. Gary Collins (1972) suggests that we are truly normal when we are at peace with God, ourselves, and others around us. God designed us for meaningful relationships in all these dimensions of life.

Models and Categories of Maladjustment

A variety of terms can be used almost interchangeably to characterize the unfortunate conditions we now consider—mental illness, emotional problems, behavior disorders, and maladjustment. All of these are labels we apply to human conditions that we regard as abnormal in some way.

The *medical model* dominates official descriptions of the various categories of mental illness. However, other views provide useful perspectives as well. The *humanistic model* blames mental illness on a social environment that blocks healthy patterns of personal growth and development. According to the *psychoanalytic model*, illness results from unresolved inner conflict and anxiety. From the perspective of the *behavioral model*, mental illness consists of learned patterns of response that are maladaptive—in other words, bad habits. For those adopting a *moral model*, unconfessed sin is the cause of emotional and mental illnesses.

Regardless of the point of view you choose, it is obvious that the various types of abnormality are manifested through distinct symptom patterns. A major task facing abnormal psychologists is to classify and describe this bewildering array of behaviors.

A group of psychopathologies occurring frequently are called *anxiety disorders*. The characteristic common to everyone suffering from one of these ailments is the experience of distressingly high levels of anxiety. One manifestation of this anxiety is in *phobias*—irrational fear of objects or situations, such as elevators or air travel, that are relatively harmless. People suffering from *panic anxiety disorder* may believe they are having a heart attack when without warning they are seized by an inexplicable sense of panic. Those who are *obsessive-compulsive* engage in ritualistic behaviors or recurring thoughts, washing their hands dozens of times a day or fretting about having left the house with the oven still on. As many as 10 percent of the population may one day suffer from some form of anxiety disorder.

A second and much less common category of pathology comprises *dissociative disorders*. People thus afflicted may experience *amnesia*, a condition marked by massive loss of memory following a traumatic event. In some cases, memory of one's personal identity—name, occupation, address, family members—

temporarily vanishes. Among the most perplexing of the disorders is a condition known as *dissociative identity disorder* in which two or more distinct personalities assume control of the same individual at different times. This condition was illustrated in the classic film *The Three Faces of Eve*.

Mood disorders comprise another group of pathologies that share the common symptom of emotional disturbance. Severe forms of *depression*, in which a person loses interest in elements of life that give it zest and meaning—eating, friends, career, sexual activity—represent one common type of mood disorder. Depression may be associated with self-destructive thoughts or suicide attempts. In some cases, periods of depression may be interspersed with intervals of near-normal emotional functioning.

A fourth cluster of pathologies is known as *personality disorders*. Chief indicators include lack of usual involvement in meaningful and stable relationships with others. People with *schizoid personality* tendencies display limited emotional responsiveness and often become withdrawn and socially isolated. Those with *antisocial personality disorder* manifest a curious lack of social sensitivity, often acting as smooth con artists who manipulate both friends and strangers for their own selfish gain.

Schizophrenia is the most debilitating and most puzzling of all the psychopathologies, and much less common than anxiety disorders. Those afflicted with schizophrenia are so severely disturbed in thought, emotion, and communication that they are incapable of carrying on normal social interactions and commitments. Some schizophrenics may be cared for at home by relatives or may continue to exist in isolation, rarely having contact with anyone. Many spend extended periods of time in psychiatric hospitals.

Having briefly described the major categories of mental illness, we now turn to the important question of the role of sin in psychopathology.

Is Mental Illness Caused by Sin?

When we observe a difficult or traumatic experience invading someone's life, we show a strong desire to find a reason for this unfortunate event. Perhaps we are acting on an unconscious hope that nothing similar will happen to us. This tendency to make unwarranted assumptions about the cause of negative experiences has a long history. When a chain of tragic events suddenly descended on the patriarch Job, his friends who came to comfort him were anxious to attribute his calamities to a flaw in Job's character. Likewise, in the account of Jesus' healing of a man born blind (John 9:1–7), the disciples' first concern was to determine whether the sin of the man himself or that of his parents was responsible for his unfortunate condition.

Psychologists specializing in mental illness are still searching for the causes of these tragic conditions. In past centuries, mental and emotional disturbances were typically attributed to the influence of evil spirits. However, that view has largely been replaced by the perspective implicit in the *medical model* of psychopathology. Mental disorders are regarded as diseases. Each new discovery of atypical patterns of brain chemistry in those with mental illness serves to strengthen the commitment of the psychiatric community to this point of view.

The medical perspective on psychopathology carries with it several powerful implications. Whether or not specific neurological roots can be identified, disorders such as depression and schizophrenia are assumed to arise from physical causes. Accurate diagnosis makes effective treatment by the experts possible, so a great deal of effort goes into categorizing and labeling these ailments correctly. In addition, the medical model suggests that we should not blame the mentally ill for their condition; instead, we should regard them with compassion, since they are victims of influences beyond their own control.

The medical model has much to commend it. Evidence for the role of genetic factors in the development of a range of mental illnesses is quite compelling. Much of the supporting data comes from the patterns of pathology found in pairs of identical twins. Additional research, particularly that on hormones and neurotransmitters, will clarify our understanding of the causes of specific illnesses. There can be no disputing the fact that biological factors play a significant part in their development.

However, the suggestion that persons who suffer from some particular mental illness bear no responsibility for their condition cannot be defended. Those who insist on eating food rich in fats increase their chances of coronary heart disease. Likewise, stress-filled lifestyles carry with them increased risk of mental illness. Although we usually do not control the events and traumas that come into our lives, we do choose how we will respond to these difficult circumstances. The attitudes and response patterns we display influence our prospects for recovery. Thus the medical model provides useful insight on mental illness, but it does not tell the whole story.

A second influential model of psychopathology is one that regards mental illness as maladaptive behavior. From a behavioral perspective, depression, phobias, and other forms of psychopathology are caused not by faulty brain chemistry, inner conflict, or moral failure. Instead, they result from learning to respond in ways that are both socially inappropriate and personally harmful. Thus, emphasis should be placed on developing more adaptive strategies for responding to whatever life may throw at the troubled individual.

There are other influential models of psychopathology besides these two, but none takes sin seriously as a possible cause of the illness. In fact, those who include reference to sin are regarded as intolerant of the rights and freedoms of others. Rarely in current psychological thinking is one's personal responsibility emphasized. Even less often is individual accountability before God taken into account. In other words, for the non-Christian psychologist seeking explanations for mental illness, sin can be safely ignored.

The Perspective of Faith

It is obvious that the concept of sin has a prominent place in Scripture. The Book of Genesis recounts how sin entered the human race through the disobedience of our first parents. In God's dealings with his chosen nation Israel, mandatory sacrifices for sin were critical. The primary purpose of Jesus' incarnation, life, death, and resurrection was to deal with the problem of human sin. Furthermore, the Bible makes it clear that the proper penalty for sin is death (Rom. 6:23) and that each of us stands guilty before God (Rom. 3:23; John 3:18). Evidently, God takes sin seriously.

But is sin the cause of all mental illness? Some Christians believe that since sin alienates us from God, mental illness cannot be dealt with until the person's relationship with God has been restored. In other words, the necessary starting point in solving any mental disorder is confession of sin and dependence on the sacrifice of Christ. Once this step has been taken, specific psychological problems, each caused by particular sinful actions or attitudes, can be resolved through confession and forgiveness.

In addition, we must consider the role of explicit influence by demonic powers on persons who manifest symptoms of psychopathology. Some Christian thinkers (Page 1989) claim that demon possession is a complex subject, but is also too important to ignore. Just as Jesus and the disciples dealt with demon possession by exorcism, so we must carefully yet decisively confront persons in whom demonic control is clearly evident.

The New Testament accounts of Jesus' life contain details of several situations in which Jesus brought healing to tormented individuals by casting out demons. (See, for example, Luke 4:31–36; 8:26–39; Matt. 15:21–28; Mark 9:14–29; Matt. 12:22–23.) In each situation, the possessed person experienced great distress together with specific physical or psychological symptoms such as violent behavior, sensory and communication loss, and seizures. At Jesus' command, the demons came out and restoration of normal functioning followed immediately.

One could propose that Jesus was mistaken in his diagnoses or was simply accommodating himself to the primitive understanding of his day. However, this position is difficult to defend (Page 1989). Alternatively, we might conclude that demon possession causes unusual behaviors that may mimic those resulting from mental illness. It would be a mistake, however, to insist that most or even many cases of psychopathology are actually unrecognized instances of demon possession.

Sall (1976) suggests several criteria by which we can distinguish mental disorders from demon possession. Two of these seem particularly critical. First, those who are demon possessed want nothing to do with Christ or any form of Christian influence. By contrast, the mentally ill are often religious and are more than willing to hear about God. Second, the recovery process is completely different. Demon-possessed persons are cured by spiritual means, with relief coming almost instantaneously. Those afflicted with mental illness normally require psychotherapy for extended periods of time.

It is clear then that sin, or at least evil spiritual powers, can produce serious emotional and behavioral problems similar to those associated with mental illness. However, these cases are best thought of as the exception rather than the rule. Even during our Lord's ministry on earth when Satan was particularly active, Jesus treated only a few human ailments as cases of demonic control. We need to explore the place of sin in pathologies of this more common type.

Putting Sin in Its Place

According to the biblical record, all human evil and suffering entered the world because of sin. Thus in one sense, every case of pathology, mental illness included, results from sin. However, just as it is unreasonable to routinely blame natural disasters or physical illness on individual human sin, it is unwise to hastily attribute mental illness to personal sin in the life of the afflicted individual. Like Job of old, this person already has more than enough to bear.

The effects of sin can be divided into at least three aspects, each of which helps account for some of the psychopathology we observe. These are personal sin, the sin of others, and the consequences of inhabiting a sinful world.

According to Ephesians 2:1, those who have not been regenerated as a result of God's grace expressed in Christ are dead in their sins. Sin is a powerful and destructive force, and those who engage in it cannot help but be affected. When we violate God's law, we reap the consequences, be they physical, psychological, or spiritual. One psychological consequence of sin is guilt. In Psalm 38, David vividly describes the distress he experienced as a result of his sin and guilt. Psychologists are well aware that unresolved guilt can lead to a host of mental and emotional disorders.

More frequently, however, one suffers as a victim of the sin of someone else. The emotional trauma experienced by victims of incest, rape, and physical or sexual abuse is caused not by a person's own sin, but by the sin of another. Their problems are clearly a result of sin, but not of personal sin.

Thirdly, the world was cursed as a result of Adam's and Eve's disobedience. To this day, we live in a world that is marred by sin and groans under the weight of God's judgment (Rom. 8:20). When, as a result of natural disasters such as floods, famine, or disease, people suffer psychological trauma, sin is once again the cause, but personal sin is not to blame. Even the inherited inclination to develop schizophrenia or depression can be thought of as part of the curse of sin on the entire created order. Many forms of psychopathology are rooted in our fallen physical and social world.

We see then that a Christian understanding of mental illness acknowledges sin as the root cause of all of our problems. However, the factors contributing to mental illness are many and varied. In his helpful discussion of the causes of abnormal behavior, Collins (1972) distinguishes between predisposing factors and precipitating factors. *Precipitating factors* refer to immediate causes, usually some sort of trauma or stress. On the other hand, *predisposing factors* include various characteristics of the person that were present prior to the onset of trauma, that is, background traits or situations. Collins argues that in both sets of factors, biological, psychological, and spiritual aspects may be involved. For example, malfunctioning glands, marital status, and lack of purpose in life can each contribute to making a specific individual vulnerable to the stress of unexpected job loss.

In conclusion, we can affirm the fact that human sinfulness is indeed responsible for mental illness. However, any simplistic account that regards the whole cause of pathology as residing in one dimension of life is bound to be unsatisfactory. Humans are marvelously complex creations; various aspects of the personality constantly interact. Jesus was committed to healing all dimensions of the individuals he encountered—body, mind, emotions, relationships, and spirits. In the same way, those who minister to the mentally ill in his name must realize they are dealing with whole persons.

Having explored the complex question of the role of sin in mental illness, we now focus on the problem of guilt. We will discover that it is crucial to distinguish between the different meanings of guilt.

Is It Good to Feel Guilty?

Practically everyone feels guilty at one time or another. One recent experience occurred when after a long weekend, I thought it was Monday (the first working day of the week) but instead it was Tuesday. As a result, a colleague who was expecting a ride home with me was left stranded, remaining on campus until 9 P.M. When I realized my error, I felt a tremendous mixture of embarrassment and guilt. Thankfully, we are still good friends!

Feelings of guilt serve a useful function in our society. Because we are not under constant observation by authority figures such as policemen or parents, we often face the temptation to behave inappropriately. A healthy sense of guilt can restrain us in those moments, and everyone benefits. In fact, some of the most dangerous members of our society are people who seem devoid of guilt feelings. They can engage in fraud, injure other people, and behave in totally selfish ways without the slightest twinge of conscience. So in modest doses, feelings of guilt are normal and valuable.

However, for many people, the burden of guilt they carry is completely out of proportion to the offenses committed, and the consequences are terribly destructive. When I inadvertently abandoned my friend, I was motivated to apologize and do everything possible to make up for my error. However, within a few days, I had almost forgotten the incident except as a humorous story to relate. If I had continued to wallow in shame and self-hatred, perhaps to the point of contemplating suicide, my guilt would have become destructive rather than adaptive.

Clinicians and counselors agree that excessive guilt is often at the root of anxiety disorders and other behavior problems. The pattern is a predictable one. A person experiences negative emotions such as strong anger, lust, or jealousy. As a result, the individual feels guilty for having these emotions. Because the sense of guilt is unpleasant, the person seeks to shun these feelings—in Freudian terms, to *repress* them. Once these feelings are pushed into the unconscious, the troubled individual is no longer aware of why guilt feelings exist and why they persist. However, symptoms of psychological distress such as depression or extreme anxiety begin to appear. By now, the guilt feelings are clearly pathological rather than beneficial. Counselors attempt to deal with this kind of inner turmoil in person after person.

Christians find the matter of guilt feelings particularly troublesome, for they often assume that these feelings have come as a result of God's conviction. However, to avoid serious confusion, we must thoughtfully examine both biblical and psychological insights and carefully define our terms.

Christian physician Paul Tournier (1962) draws an important distinction between true and false guilt. He suggests that *true guilt* results from a breakdown in our proper relationship to God—one of complete trust and dependency. *False guilt*, while no less real in terms of our feelings, arises when we violate human expectations, often those of our parents. These standards may have little or no relation to the laws of God.

Narramore (1984) expresses a similar distinction in *No Condemnation* in a slightly different way. According to Narramore, *objective guilt* reflects our standing before God. It is almost totally independent of our feelings. We may seriously violate his commands, yet have no sense of guilt, or we may be burdened with unrelenting feelings of guilt that do not contribute to God's purposes for us. Narramore uses the term *subjective guilt* to identify our feelings as distinct from our status in the eyes of God. When the Bible speaks about guilt, Narramore maintains, it is always *objective guilt*, the kind based on our standing before God. (See, for example, 1 John 3:19–20.) However, when psychologists work with troubled clients, they seek to help people cope with *subjective guilt*, their feelings of self-criticism and hatred. Dealing with excessive feelings of guilt may restore a greater degree of psychological health, but it does nothing to change a person's standing before God. It is not intended to do so.

Therefore, in considering how we can deal with guilt, we must clearly distinguish between our feelings and our standing before God. Subjective guilt (or guilt feelings) dwells on past actions and is focused on the self. Objective guilt looks toward the future and is other-oriented. Its concern is with how others are affected, rather than with how miserable I may feel. The two have different origins and need to be dealt with in totally different ways.

For people plagued with unrealistic, persistent, and debilitating feelings of guilt, the recommendations of Leo Madow (1988) are worth heeding. He suggests the following steps:

1. Become aware of your guilt feelings, particularly if they have been denied in the past.
2. Accept the fact that your negative feelings (anger, jealousy, etc.) are legitimate, although it may not be appropriate to act on these feelings.
3. Review the standards by which you are judging yourself to see if they are realistic. Self-forgiveness may be needed.
4. Examine your conscience. It should not condemn you after you have attempted to make things right.
5. Make restitution for your actions if you have not yet done so.
6. If intense guilt persists, seek professional help.

Madow's suggestions contain a great deal of practical wisdom. Guilt feelings are often generated when parents and other authority figures impose impossible standards on impressionable youngsters. Unable to reason that these standards are inappropriate, children have few options but to adopt them, even though they bring intense guilt feelings. The sense of self-condemnation is neither necessary nor helpful, for guilt is a poor motivator. It more often paralyzes the one burdened with it than spurs the person to corrective action.

But what about real, objective guilt? Psychologists and counselors have neither the inclination nor the authority to deliver any of us from true guilt. For that, we must look to a different source.

Christian counselor Bruce Narramore (1984) maintains that feelings of guilt—at least the extreme debilitating kind—find no place in Scripture. Christians are mistaken when they associate strong feelings of guilt with conviction from the Holy Spirit. In fact, Narramore argues, the self-condemnation brought about by a strong sense of guilt is often harmful both psychologically and spiritually. Such an attitude may reflect an effort to earn salvation through self-atonement, rather than depending wholly on the provision of Christ. It may prevent the person from honestly admitting his complete inability to deal with his own sin.

What then is the alternative to guilt and self-depreciation? Narramore calls it *godly sorrow*. According to 2 Corinthians 7:10, godly sorrow leads to repentance, whereas worldly sorrow (feelings of guilt) results in death. As long as we refuse to depend on Christ alone for forgiveness, we are without hope. It is only as we realize the amazing depth of God's love for us that we are moved to cast ourselves on his mercy and find true forgiveness.

The distinction between these two kinds of guilt is an important one. Persistent feelings of guilt focus on past failures, but godly sorrow is oriented toward changed patterns in the future. Feelings of guilt are almost totally self-directed, while godly sorrow focuses on the one who has been offended. Perhaps the clearest example of the difference is seen in the lives of two of Jesus' disciples, Judas and Peter. Each was guilty of a terrible sin, but the subsequent course each charted was completely different. Judas's horrible sense of guilt and shame was directed inward, and it became unbearable. In his despair, Judas took his own life. Peter likewise felt great remorse, but as he realized how deeply he had wronged his Lord, he was motivated by a sense of God's limitless love to repent and make a new start. The contrast could not be more striking.

Reflecting Back

Throughout our discussion of the causes and characteristics of mental illness, the key word is **isolation**. Those unfortunate persons who display abnormal behaviors are isolated from other people because they do not communicate effectively or because they are misunderstood. Often they are separated from their own feelings as well as from the world around them. In addition, they may feel alienated from God.

After pondering the meaning of normality, we explored the role of sin in mental illness. We concluded that while personal sin is the cause of some but by no means all psychological problems, sin in the broader sense is indeed to blame for all human pathology. Much of the suffering is caused by the sin of others. As well, we are often affected by the context in which we live—a planet that continues to groan under the judgment God pronounced upon it when sin entered human experience.

Finally, we considered the important and universal experience of guilt. Having distinguished between objective and subjective guilt, we concluded that feelings of guilt need to be faced realistically, perhaps with the help of a sensitive counselor. True guilt, on the other hand, results from violating the law of God and can be addressed only when we turn to him in repentance and godly sorrow. Thankfully, ours is a God of great mercy and compassion.

Going Deeper

1. For a helpful treatment of the subject of guilt, read Bruce Narramore's *No Condemnation* (Zondervan, 1984).
2. A good discussion of feelings of guilt and how to deal with the pain they bring is found in Leo Madow's *Guilt: How to Recognize and Cope with It* (Jason Aronson, 1988).
3. For a consideration of the place of demon possession in mental illness, read "Demon possession or psychopathology? A clinical differentiation" by M. J. Sall, *Journal of Psychology and Theology* 4 (1976): 286–90.
4. For a balanced discussion of the complex causes of mental illness, consult chapter 1 of Gary Collins's *Fractured Personalities* (Creation House, 1972).
5. For an inside look at the bewildering illness of schizophrenia, read Carol North's *Welcome Silence* (Simon and Schuster, 1987).

11

Therapy and Health

Early in my teaching career, I had my one and only serious battle with depression. Having signed a contract for an exciting new position at the other end of the country, I was scheduled to begin my new job in September. In the meantime, I had agreed to stay on and teach a summer course in introductory psychology to help pay our moving costs.

The first class meeting was three hours long on a Monday evening early in May, and there were 280 students enrolled. Despite being a rookie instructor, I survived that first session—it went surprisingly well. But for the rest of that week I was too depressed to care about anything. I did not look forward to my teaching, something that I normally enjoy thoroughly; I wasn't even excited about the upcoming relocation and new position. For the next four or five days, my whole world seemed to be painted in a dull grey.

I am thankful to report that as mysteriously as it had descended, my depression began to lift about a week later. However, I have never forgotten that thick cloud of despair through which I groped for several days.

Friends, Helpers, and Psychotherapists

Periodically, we each face challenges that tax our coping capacities to the limit. At times like these, the value of a good friend is hard to measure. Experiences like discovering you have a serious illness, receiving an unexpected repair bill you don't have the money to pay, or having a heated argument with someone close to you seem to be an inescapable part of life. However, these curves in the road are easier to navigate when somebody who cares is traveling with you.

Some of us are reluctant to become involved in *psychotherapy* (also known as professional counseling) because we see this as an admission of failure. There is a certain stigma attached to seeking professional help. But what is psychotherapy? One thoughtful counselor has described it this way: "Psychotherapy is, at root, self-disclosure to a wise and understanding advisor" (Worthington 1982, 184). In that sense, it is not so different from unloading your troubles on a friend. In fact, a less complementary capsule description of psychotherapy is "rent-a-friend" (Bobgan and Bobgan 1979, 160). Is a friend we rent better than one we get for nothing?

A sympathetic friend with a listening ear can be a marvelous gift from God when you face one of life's heavy blows. Unlike a professional counselor who you probably see only during regularly scheduled visits, a good friend offers an established relationship that will continue long after the present crisis has passed. In addition, he or she is probably more similar to you than your psychotherapist is, and has the advantage of understanding how you function in a variety of contexts (Worthington 1982).

Although the help of a good friend is often sufficient, there are times when the necessary commitment of emotional resources, time, and specialized insight is too much to ask of a friend. When you face a persistent or a particularly serious problem, seeing a trained counselor has numerous advantages. A psychotherapist offers genuine caring and empathy, but at the same time is able to be more objective about your struggles than a friend can be. An experienced therapist has the advantage of working with other people in similar situations and of learning which strategies are most likely to be effective. A psychotherapist can accurately judge the seriousness of your problem and determine the kind of treatment likely to be helpful. In addition, as a result of extensive training in personality dynamics, a professional counselor can often lead you into deeper self-understanding. Therapists and friends—we need both, but at different times and in different situations.

A Range of Therapeutic Interventions

All psychotherapeutic interventions are aimed at restoring or enhancing a person's mental and emotional health. Regardless of the specific therapy applied, counseling is always based on personal interactions between therapists and their clients. These relationships are probably the most significant components of therapy. Clearly, they provide one of the common threads that runs through a wide variety of approaches. Though there are dozens of specific brands of therapy in use, we can consider only a few. These will be sufficient to show how the various approaches reflect diverse views of human nature and functioning.

Psychoanalysis is both a personality theory (see the discussion in chapter 9) and a major approach to therapy. Freud maintained that inner conflict is an inescapable part of human experience. Difficulties arise when conflicts and memories too painful to face are pushed out of consciousness. The therapist's task is to help clients gain insight into persistent problems by probing the unconscious mind in which troublesome fears, memories, and conflicts are buried. Through a combination of methods, therapists guide their patients toward fuller self-understanding and the ability to deal with their anxieties realistically.

A popular form of therapy developed by Carl Rogers is called *person-centered therapy*. Rogers held a positive view of human potential and capacity for growth. He believed that the therapist's most important function is to provide understanding and acceptance—often called *unconditional positive regard*. Affirmation and empathy are communicated primarily through the therapist functioning as a psychological mirror, reflecting and helping to clarify the person's thoughts and feelings. This kind of active listening is essential if the person is to find the courage to deal honestly with present anxieties and future challenges.

In order to deal with inappropriate actions or destructive habits, *behavior therapy* is often employed. This approach is based on the assumption that problem behaviors have been learned through classical and operant conditioning (discussed in chapter 5). They need to be *unlearned* by similar means. The therapist uses mutually planned programs of rewards or punishments to assist the client in altering troublesome patterns of behavior.

As the name suggests, *cognitive therapies* attempt to solve people's problems by changing the way they think about them. For example, Albert Ellis, who developed *rational-emotive therapy*, argues that a person's beliefs are often irrational—they do not line up with the facts of one's life situation. Because these beliefs and perceptions are distorted, the individual often reacts to problems in self-defeating ways. The solution lies in coming to perceive challenging situations in more accurate and realistic ways.

Distinct from any of the approaches we have considered so far are a group of *biological treatments* that involve intervening medically through drugs or surgery. These methods of therapy assume a physical cause for one's disorder, usually a malfunctioning in the brain. Psychiatrists (professionals who have both medical and psychological training) often implement drug therapies when they suspect that chemical imbalances exist. This type of treatment may occur either by itself or in conjunction with one of those already discussed.

There have been many debates, some of them emotionally charged, over the extent to which therapeutic interventions are effective in resolving mental and emotional problems. It turns out to be surprisingly difficult to assess the effectiveness of therapy, partly because the appropriate criteria for judging success are not clear. Naturally, counselors want to believe that their efforts are worthwhile, so unbiased assessment of their own success is difficult for them. A general conclusion is that a wide variety of therapies can be helpful. However, the degree of benefit to be gained depends on the nature of the problem and on the skill and sensitivity of the therapist as well as on the method used.

Any individual who feels the need for professional help must decide on a suitable therapist. For Christians, one significant dimension of this choice is the question of whether to seek help from a non-Christian or a Christian therapist. To this important issue we now turn.

Should a Christian Visit a Non-Christian Therapist?

Current forms of psychotherapy come in a confusing array of styles and colors. One recent estimate places the number of distinct therapies in use at 250! The general types that we have reviewed constitute only a small sample of those available. No doubt, more new ones will be developed in coming months.

Among Christian counselors, there is also a wide variety of therapeutic approaches. Some practitioners develop their own distinct methods of counseling, while others adapt and modify secular approaches such as Gestalt therapy or person-centered therapy. They may incorporate biblical concepts and insights into existing methods. But counseling done by Christians is no more homogeneous than counseling in general.

Psychologists who conduct research often study counseling methods and techniques, and they sometimes compare the effectiveness of different approaches. However, this research has had almost no influence on the therapeutic methods themselves. As McLemore points out, "psychotherapy is more art than science" (1982, 26). The diversity of approaches reflects both the complexity of human nature and the varying personalities and life experiences of the counselors who develop them.

Concerns about the appropriateness of a Christian being counseled by an unbelieving therapist arise primarily from two sources. The first is the fact that every major brand of therapy was created by someone who rejected a Christian world view. Freud, Skinner, and Rogers each developed a counseling approach that fits his particular understanding of people, an understanding that was not based on biblical insight. Therefore, it is not surprising that some of the perspectives contained in these approaches run counter to a biblical understanding of human nature.

The second source of concern is the fact that the moral, ethical, and personal values held by any counselor will come through in interactions with clients. Regardless of the particular counseling method employed, the beliefs and priorities of counselors will be conveyed in the goals they set, the advice they give, and the criteria of recovery they apply. There is clearly potential for a clash in value systems when a believer seeks advice from a non-Christian counselor.

The reason why you might consider visiting a non-Christian counselor is not hard to understand. Life's stresses and challenges come to us in a wide variety of forms, and the reasons for seeking help from a therapist are diverse. The specialized training and experience of counselors also varies widely. One would not be referred to the same medical specialist for treatment of hormonal imbalances, lower back pain, and infection of the inner ear. In the same way, no one psychotherapist is likely to be an expert in marriage counseling, child sexual abuse, and mood disorders. It is natural to seek help from the best qualified person, and that person might be an unbeliever. When that is the case, you as a potential client face a difficult choice.

The Perspective of Faith

A friend of mine has a deliberate policy that he applies consistently when he needs services of any kind—house repair, legal advice, or a new appliance. He always tries to patronize a fellow believer. This may not be unusual for Christians, but my friend's reason for doing so is unique: God's work needs money to operate, and if a Christian earns it, God is more likely to receive his tithe! The logic is hard to dispute.

Because Christian counselors can better appreciate the importance I place on my relationship with God and my moral values, I prefer them over similarly trained and experienced unbelievers. But is it wise to categorically rule out the option of seeking help from a non-Christian?

In order to investigate this question more thoroughly, we need to think about what Christian counseling involves. By now, you should not be surprised that Christians take different positions on this matter. For some, it means using the Bible and nothing more as one's basis for understanding the problem, setting goals for counseling, and suggesting how those goals can best be reached. Jay Adams (1971) is known for his insistence that believers have no need for psychological training in order to be *Competent to Counsel*.

Other equally committed Christians regard the psychological and spiritual dimensions of life as separate from each other. Thus, if an individual has a problem rooted in spiritual concerns such as guilt over the violation of biblical standards, the person needs biblically based counseling, perhaps from a pastor. However, when a person suffers from a psychological problem such as excessive anxiety, the individual should see a psychologist. For difficulties rooted in mental and emotional realms, biblical insights are seen as irrelevant.

Although both of these views are held by true Christians, neither is a good example of Christian counseling. The former is better thought of as pastoral counseling, a form of ministry that has usually been practiced in churches and that continues to be important. It is not, however, counseling in the sense in which we are using the term. The second view, one that compartmentalizes spiritual and psychological concerns, does not lead to uniquely Christian approaches to therapy, for it is based almost entirely on insights derived from secular psychology. Neither position provides the depth of helpful counsel that is available through applying psychological insight in the context of a biblical understanding of persons and human problems. This third approach, one that is based on a biblically informed psychology, is what is meant by *Christian counseling.*

What exactly are the distinctives of Christian counseling or psychotherapy? Although we will not agree on all its elements, several aspects are typical. First, Christian counseling is based on a biblical view of the person. It therefore considers the whole person, including spiritual or religious dimensions. In his intriguing work *Putting the Soul Back in Psychology*, psychiatrist John White (1987) makes a strong case for the fact that all people are intrinsically and incurably religious. Secular counseling approaches minimize or even deny our essential spiritual nature, and therefore operate on a faulty premise. Christian counseling is based on consideration of all the dimensions of human personality—physical, emotional, mental, relational, and spiritual.

A related distinctive, one suggested by Cosgrove and Mallory (1977), is that Christian counselors will distinguish between healthy and neurotic aspects of religious belief. In the opinion of many secular counselors, all religious beliefs are harmful, for they prevent growth and wholeness by placing burdens of unnecessary guilt on those who adopt them. A Christian counselor recognizes that religious commitments may interfere with psychological health, especially when they involve externally imposed standards divorced from an understanding of the love of God. However, as we will see later in this chapter, spiritual commitment and emotional health can be complementary.

A third characteristic of Christian counseling is that it is built on the guidance of the Holy Spirit and focused on Christ (Worthington 1982). A Christian counselor will seek wisdom and insight relevant to a particular client's need from God through prayer and study of the Scriptures. This approach recognizes that just as physicians cooperate with God in bringing physical healing, so Christian psychotherapists are working together with God in attempting to bring wholeness within the personalities of hurting people. Human and divine influences are both involved.

Finally, Christian counseling will be partially distinctive in its goals. As Benner and Palmer express it, "The goals of the Christian therapist must be both immediate and ultimate" (1986, 175). In the short range, a client's symptoms need to be addressed and relieved. It is a matter of integrity that the client's expectation for counseling rather than evangelism be respected. At the same time, however, Christian psychotherapists are convinced of the fact that no individual can be fully whole without being restored to relationship with the Creator. Thus, they will be alert for evidence that their clients may be searching for answers to life's ultimate questions, as well as struggling with more immediate concerns.

Making an Informed Choice

To be a Christian therapist in the sense in which we have been using the term is a demanding task. One needs both a thorough grasp of the principles of Scripture and a good understanding of the best psychological theories and techniques available. In addition, a Christian counselor needs to have compassion for human need of all kinds and a deep desire to see people grow in all dimensions of life.

Meier et al. (1991, 336) propose that the following specific qualities are essential for Christian counselors:

1. an ability to accept people unconditionally,
2. skill in listening with interest and warmth,
3. knowledge of various counseling techniques and when to use each,
4. sensitivity in the use of prayer and Scripture,
5. capacity to accept without alarm whatever they are told,
6. ability to inspire realistic confidence and optimism, and
7. a good sense of humor.

In considering seeking help from either a fellow believer or a non-Christian counselor, one would look for a professional with many of these qualities. It is wise to ask questions about a potential therapist's training, experience, and orientation before making a commitment. Do not hesitate to request names of both fellow therapists and former clients who can help you assess the suitability of a particular counselor for your present need. Consider whether this person has worked with clients with similar concerns, and ask how they were dealt with. If possible, talk with some of these people. Request a written statement of the therapist's training, credentials, and religious and philosophical views. There is more at stake here than getting a tune-up for your car, so the extra effort is well worth it. Along with all this, seek advice from trusted friends and ask God to direct you to someone uniquely gifted to work effectively with you.

Mental Health and the Believer

In North American society, concerns with health—physical, emotional, and mental—are near the top of our list of priorities. The elusive pursuit of youthfulness, vitality, and holistic health continues at a frenzied pace, and the prospect of aging becomes increasingly threatening. We want not just to avoid illness, but to be fully healthy.

This emphasis on health, especially mental and emotional health, has intriguing implications for Christians. In fact, health and wholeness thinking is present in the Christian church in the form of the *health-and-wealth gospel*. This perspective interprets Scripture selectively to suggest that God's children can expect to enjoy a life of health, comfort, and material prosperity. According to some, we should all be living like King's Kids!

The relationship between mental health and Christian faith is worthy of our thoughtful reflections. Abraham Maslow made extensive studies of people considered to be most healthy, most fully human. He described them as having realistic perceptions of themselves, as displaying creativity and spontaneity, as being other-oriented, and as enjoying satisfying interpersonal relationships (Cosgrove and Mallory 1977). All of these characteristics seem to be reasonable indicators of mental health.

The aspect of healthy people being other-oriented or altruistic is particularly intriguing, for it clearly parallels Christian teaching and Jesus' example. There can scarcely be a more altruistic act than giving one's life for someone else. It is also worthy of note that self-preoccupation is characteristic of many emotional disturbances. With therapy and restored health come an increased capacity to be aware of and respond to the concerns of others. Our inveterate self-centeredness is a powerful manifestation of our fallen human nature.

Examining mental health from a Christian perspective, Grounds (1976) identified three essential ingredients, without which one cannot be mentally healthy. One is a deep conviction that life has meaning. Without this, there will be little motivation or purpose for day-to-day activities. The second is courage to face the many challenges that life brings. Though we are occasionally fearful, perhaps even terrified with what lies ahead, it is clearly unhealthy to feel constantly overwhelmed by what we face. Thirdly, to be healthy, one must be able to both give and receive love. This implies the presence of stable, meaningful, and satisfying relationships. We were created by God for relationships, and without them we are clearly less than human.

It is worth pointing out that another person's level of mental health cannot be readily judged. In fact, this characteristic can be assessed only on the basis of long-term patterns of response in a variety of situations. Thus, mental and emotional health is demonstrated as one copes with a variety of life's challenges and rebounds successfully from its misfortunes. A healthy person is strengthened rather than destroyed by these events.

Although we must not equate the notions of mental health and spiritual maturity, it is clear that they are often linked. The fact that good emotional adjustment can be nurtured by Christian faith is evident when we reflect on the three ingredients of mental health identified earlier—meaning, courage, and love. More specifically, faith in God and a sense of his calling on one's life can provide meaning and purpose. To be asked by the infinite Creator to carry out a specific task certainly offers a profound sense of purpose. Second, the security of belonging to God and being indwelt by his Spirit is an excellent antidote to fear and timidity (2 Tim. 1:7). Finally, the context of God's family, the body of Christ, in which we share equal status with other believers as children of God, is a natural place to love others and in turn to be loved.

Despite the fact that mental and spiritual health are logically related, it is obvious that exceptions to these patterns exist. According to McLemore (1982), when the usual standards of mental health are applied, Christians look neither better nor worse than anyone else. In addition, many people with no Christian faith or religious commitment are judged to be mentally healthy. Why are the links between faith and health not closer?

Three points need to be considered in coming to a clearer understanding. First, even though faith in God has potential for mental and emotional health benefits, a Christian may not take advantage of them. This could occur because of an inaccurate view of God and a lack of trust in him, such that the person would not make a complete personal commitment to God. Probably few of us appropriate all the blessings that are available to us as children of God.

In addition, there is a sense in which the standards of mental and emotional health that are customarily applied are flawed standards. For example, in the thinking of a believer, a sense of one's own sinfulness is healthy and right. Indeed, as White (1987) reminds us, every person who truly encounters God is overwhelmed by God's holiness and his own contrasting sinfulness. Isaiah and John the apostle are good biblical examples. To the unbeliever, awareness of one's own sin might well be regarded as pathological guilt, a sure indication of poor mental health.

Third, we need to remember that as Christians, we are citizens of another world; we do not belong here. Consequently, there is a degree of tension arising simply from the discrepant values and ideals that a Christian espouses. These may contribute to reduced mental health, at least in the sense it is normally understood. The expectation that God's children will be healthy and well-adjusted is perhaps less of a biblically derived standard than an infiltration of secular values into our thinking. We do after all inhabit a fallen and sin-cursed world.

In reflecting on the matter of mental health, we need to ask whether health and wellness are appropriate goals for Christians to pursue. This is an important consideration, for it brings us face to face with the question of whether enhancing a person's emotional health, perhaps through counseling, without leading him or her to salvation through faith in Christ, is wise use of the believer's time and energy. McLemore offers this opinion: "To take the edge off someone's despair without at least nodding in the direction of Christ may be, in the long run, to do that person a disservice" (1982, 173).

Certainly, all believers need to be ready to communicate the reason for their hope when God opens another person's heart. However, there is also clear evidence in Scripture that God is concerned for the total person, not just saving the soul. For example, Jesus sometimes brought healing to people's bodies or emotions when we have no indication that their eternal destiny was altered by this encounter. We are challenged to meet the needs of others as we "weep with those who weep" (Rom. 12:15), "carry each other's burdens" (Gal. 6:2), and "help the weak" (1 Thess. 5:14). True religion as defined in James 1:27 has a practical component of compassion for those who hurt.

All of these considerations regarding the importance of health and healing for the whole person need to be understood in God's perspective. He is never in a hurry and is always seeking to restore the wayward through his limitless love and grace. His heart of compassion is moved with our distresses, and he has one overriding purpose in our lives. This is not our mental health, good adjustment, or freedom from trouble. It is that we be "conformed to the likeness of his Son" (Rom. 8:29). Other concerns such as those for emotional healing are not unimportant—they are just not most important.

In his ministry among us, Jesus healed many, restoring full humanity in every possible dimension. However, he did not promise health and comfort to his followers. Our first commitment must be to serve God and to reach out to others. Southard sums it up effectively: "Mental health is a by-product of surrender to values higher than ourselves" (1972, 22).

Reflecting Back

Throughout the discussions of this chapter, our emphasis has been on **wholeness**. Both interested friends and trained psychotherapists seek to restore unity and completeness in the fractured and fragmented lives of hurting people. We reviewed a variety of prominent approaches to therapy, noting that the personal relationship between the therapist and client is crucial, regardless of the techniques employed.

In debating whether Christians should seek help from non-Christian therapists, we noted the diversity of approaches employed by both groups of counselors. We also identified several distinctives of Christian counseling, noting that not all Christians who counsel conduct genuine Christian counseling. While we would prefer to receive help from a fellow believer, we must at least find a counselor who understands and respects our beliefs and values. The chosen therapist should also have a high level of experience and competence in the area of our need.

Finally, we discussed the relationship between mental and spiritual health. We admitted that while faith in God may enhance mental health, this is not the experience of all believers. For a variety of reasons, faith and emotional health are often not linked closely. God cares for the whole person, but his first concern is our growth in likeness to Christ.

Going Deeper

1. For an overview of a Christian view on counseling and mental health, read Mark Cosgrove's and James Mallory's *Mental Health: A Christian Approach* (Zondervan, 1977).
2. For an inspiring reminder of the importance of the spiritual dimension, I recommend John White's *Putting the Soul Back in Psychology* (InterVarsity, 1987).

3. For guidance on offering practical counseling help, you might consult Everett Worthington's *When Someone Asks for Help* (InterVarsity, 1982).
4. For a thoughtful treatment of the tensions between faith and counseling, I recommend Clinton McLemore's *The Scandal of Psychotherapy* (Tyndale House, 1982).
5. For a brief Christian critique of counseling approaches and a description of the distinctives of Christian counseling, read chapter 8 of Stan Jones's *Psychology and the Christian Faith* (Baker, 1986).

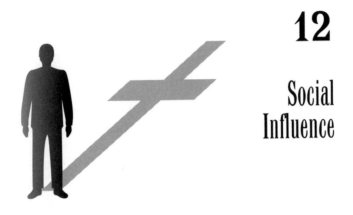

12

Social Influence

April 19, 1993 was a black day in Waco, Texas. Seven weeks earlier, the United States Bureau of Alcohol, Tobacco, and Firearms (ATF) had raided the headquarters of a religious cult known as the Branch Davidians. The purpose of this raid was to confiscate illegal weapons and to arrest David Koresh, the leader of the cult. However, in the ensuing gun battle, four ATF agents and six cult members were killed. At that point, the Federal Bureau of Investigation (FBI) stepped in.

Initially content to wait and to work toward a peaceful settlement, FBI officials attempted to negotiate with cult leaders. Early in the siege, Koresh promised he would surrender, but as days stretched into weeks, the authorities grew increasingly impatient. On the morning of April 19, the FBI took decisive action. Large holes were punched in the compound walls, and tear gas was sprayed intermittently on the buildings inside. However, a few hours after the assault began, fire unexpectedly erupted in several sections of the compound at the same time. In a matter of minutes, the wooden structures were destroyed, and as many as eighty-two cult members, a number of them children, died in the flames. David Koresh was among them.

Who was responsible for the tragedy at Waco? Had Koresh been planning a mass suicide all along? Did the authorities act with unnecessary haste and excessive force? The debate will probably continue for a long time. One thing is certain: On both sides of the conflict, specific individuals wielded tremendous influence over others. Such is the nature of human existence.

Random Acts of Kindness

Fortunately, the influence people exert on one another is not always destructive. A lady once stopped at a highway toll booth and paid the fee for the next six drivers (Lara 1992). As each of them approached the booth, they were greeted by an unusually cheery toll collector: "Someone has already paid your fare—have a good day!" Now that's an unexpected treat!

You may have been the recipient of simple yet unexpected kindnesses in other situations. Perhaps you were anxiously waiting in line to see your bank teller when, for no apparent reason, the customer ahead of you volunteered to let you go first. Alternatively, suppose that you have been driving around the grocery store parking lot for nearly fifteen minutes looking for a parking spot. Finally you see an empty space just ahead, only to realize that another driver has reached it first. Then, to your amazement and delight, this stranger cheerfully offers to let you take the space while she keeps looking!

Unprovoked acts of kindness such as these can have a remarkable impact on their recipients. Suddenly, the world becomes a little less hostile, and the spark of faith in human nature is rekindled. Chances are that because of the positive mindset it engenders, the kindness received will be passed on, perhaps in a totally different form. Who knows where the chain of good will might lead? In addition, the giver also reaps the rewards of having brightened someone else's day.

Random acts of kindness—a simple but powerful principle. Although it may have been rediscovered only recently, the concept has a long history. Two thousand years ago, Jesus instructed his followers, "Do to others as you would have them do to you" (Luke 6:31). If more of us followed the *golden rule*, the world would be a better place.

Attraction, Attitudes, and Altruism

Humans are inherently social, and our interactions with others form an essential dimension of life. It is the ways in which individuals are influenced by others that social psychologists choose to investigate. Although we affect one another in a myriad of ways, several of those ways have been the focus of careful study.

Each of us finds certain people appealing, and others offensive or at least uninteresting. These positive and negative responses are the stuff of love and hate, of friendship and interpersonal clash, of satisfying relationships and exhausted patience. What causes us to be attracted to certain other people? Among the factors psychologists have identified are similarity, physical appearance, and proximity. Thus, if you want someone to like you, choose a person with whom you share similar interests and values; make yourself look neat and attractive; and make sure you cross paths repeatedly!

Social psychologists also deal with attitudes—how they are formed and how they can be changed. Although we typically assume that our attitudes—religious, political, racial—control our actions, research suggests that the link is much weaker than we might expect. Conversely, one of the most effective ways to create a shift in attitude is to first induce a change in behavior. We will explore some fascinating applications of this dynamic principle later in the chapter.

Conformity and compliance refer to more direct influence that other people have on us. With a group of friends, we often feel pressure to conform even though we may not agree, perhaps out of fear of rejection. An authority figure giving orders we don't like can elicit a surprising degree of compliance from us. One of psychology's most famous studies—Stanley Milgram's investigation of obedience to authority—illustrates this fact dramatically.

Why do passers-by usually not offer help to someone in need? Studies of bystander intervention show that we are surprisingly reluctant to help, especially when other apparently apathetic people are present. For a variety of reasons, *good Samaritans* are hard to find.

In a world increasingly becoming a global village, we come in frequent contact with people of different cultures, languages, and customs. Thus social psychologists' investigations of stereotypes and prejudice are of growing relevance. Intercultural tensions are at the root of much conflict and suffering in our world. Reconciliation between diverse groups and individuals is facilitated by an understanding of others' uniqueness and by working together toward a common goal. Racially mixed sports teams are but one example.

In seeking to account for someone's behavior, be it praiseworthy or disgusting, we have two choices. We can attribute the behavior to either the situational factors (the surrounding physical or social environment) or dispositional ones (qualities of character or personality within the individual). Research has consistently shown that in explaining others' behavior, we are too willing to blame the person's inner qualities, even though situational factors may be compelling. We quite readily blame our own actions on the situation, especially if we have behaved inappropriately. When I drive too fast, this is because I had to make an important appointment; when other people speed, they are reckless drivers. Not entirely fair, is it?

Understanding the influences we have on each other is an important goal for social psychologists. Having made progress in this regard, however, we face the challenge of using that knowledge wisely. To this issue we now turn.

Social Influence: Manipulation or Stewardship?

Christians are called to influence those around them. Jesus used the metaphors of salt and light (Matt. 5:13–16) to illustrate the way in which we should shape the surrounding society. In the proclamation of the good news of God's love and grace, we help to bring about profound changes in people's lives. We are indeed called to change our world.

The following letter illustrates one way of attempting to influence another person.

My Dear Brother Jones,

God has just laid your name upon my heart and I feel led to send you this very special *prayer square*. I am enclosing the testimony of Mr. Smith whom God blessed with a $150,000 per year job and two new Cadillacs after he used the prayer square. Follow the directions, and when you have finished, send the prayer square back to me so that I can rush it to the next dear soul in need.

Please place your gift on the X on the square when you send it back so that our family can continue to fight to keep this land safe for our children. Thousands of others are standing with you in support of this poor country boy fighting the forces of evil. Just remember, any gift however small will help.

This is a fictitious letter, but it contains elements of letters many of us have received. It also illustrates several influence techniques that are widely used and quite effective. Here are a few of them:

Card-stacking is the selection of only those examples that support the influencer's argument. Mr. Smith's experience of prosperity is presented as if it were typical.

Plain folks refers to the association of the product with simple, naive people. Note the phrase *this poor country boy.*

A *testimonial* involves use of a specific personal case that illustrates successful application of the proponent's argument. Mr. Smith is presented as a real person.

The *bandwagon* effect results from the impression that many other people are involved. The letter claimed that "thousands of others are standing with you."

The *foot-in-the-door* technique involves first asking the person to take a small step of support and cooperation in order to make the person more willing to agree to a larger request. Having read the letter, used the square, or sent in a small gift, the recipient would be more willing to make larger donations in the future.

Name calling is a way of persuading someone to reject something they know little about. In the letter, anything associated with the "forces of evil" should clearly be rejected.

Financial appeals are not the only way in which certain individuals seek to influence many others. Christians often apply influence techniques in asking people to come forward to indicate their newly made commitment to Christ. If this initial step is followed by further requests such as joining a group of new disciples, *foot-in-the-door* methods are at work. If pastoral staff or lay counselors come forward in substantial numbers when the appeal is made, the *bandwagon* effect comes into play. In addition, the direct effects of modeling (discussed in chapter 4) are also involved. Each of these increases a person's willingness to respond by coming forward.

These means of influencing others are certainly not unique to evangelical Christian settings. A wide range of techniques are applied by religious cults such as the Branch Davidians, as well as in many facets of business and sales. In all these situations, the techniques are powerful and effective. The issue with which we must deal is whether Christians ought to employ them.

The Perspective of Faith

For those wishing to support the use of social influence techniques in Christian causes, compelling arguments can be presented. Christians have always taken advantage of cultural and scientific developments to more effectively spread the gospel. First developed in the fifteenth century, printing presses have made Bibles widely available. Mass media such as radio and television have been extensively used for religious programming, both in America and around the world. Mission Aviation Fellowship relies heavily on aircraft and communications technology to effectively serve a range of Christian organizations. Wycliffe Bible translators make extensive use of sophisticated computer software in linguistic and translation work. In these and other applications we might name, the techniques involved are tools to be harnessed for a good cause. More effective means of persuading people to listen to the gospel have similar positive potential.

A related point in favor of employing social influence techniques in Christian causes is that the techniques themselves are neutral. The same presses that print Bibles can also be used to produce pornography or pamphlets that stir up hatred. In a similar fashion, influence methods may be used for selling junk food or luring hungry people into dangerous cults, as well as for persuading those in spiritual need to listen to the message of God's love and forgiveness.

One final supporting perspective derives from the simple fact that influence techniques are everywhere. They are already being widely used for a multitude of causes, often in unsystematic ways. Social influence is a fact of life. To refuse to apply its techniques in the church is a restrictive and unnecessary limitation that gains nothing and undermines the effectiveness of Christian organizations.

Despite these important benefits, however, we need to examine the other side of the coin. Deliberate application of social influence techniques in the church may carry with it some hidden dangers. One area of concern has to do with misplaced emphasis. While we are called to influence our culture, we do this primarily through living in obedience to God and proclaiming the good news. It is God's responsibility rather than ours to change the hearts of people.

Secondly, when influence techniques are used deliberately, they become little more than thinly veiled manipulation. As such they have potential for abuse, for the associated power may corrupt its users and lead them to pursue less worthy ends. As well, manipulation frequently backfires, eliciting scorn and cynicism rather than a positive response from its recipients.

Finally, reliance on psychological tricks reveals a lack of faith in God. Scripture is clear that human effort by itself has limited benefit (Ps. 127:1). In his own evangelistic ministry, Paul was careful not to rely on the human skill and wisdom that he had at his disposal (1 Cor. 2:1–5). His reason was clear—he wanted the changed lives of his hearers to be grounded in the power of God rather than in human influence.

Cautious Affirmation

The issues we are considering merit prayerful and thoughtful consideration by all those involved in Christian causes. It is critical that we correctly understand our role as co-laborers with God (1 Cor. 3:5–9). While each one has a significant part to play, it is God who is responsible for any lasting results.

The twin dangers of taking too much or too little initiative continually lurk as we seek to participate in building the kingdom. God is sovereign, yet throughout history, he has chosen to accomplish his purposes through frail and fallible humans. This is evident in the imperfect lives of Jacob, Rahab, Nehemiah, and Paul, as well as dozens of other people of God, both ancient and contemporary. The best of human organization and skill is appropriate, but it is never sufficient to accomplish God's purposes. We have the privilege of participating in what God is doing.

Clearly, our motives come into play when we consider the methods to be employed in doing God's work. While our ability to judge our own motives is limited, we can ask God to search our hearts (Ps. 139:23–24), including our motivations. In addition, it is wise to seek advice from trusted friends who can objectively assess the appropriateness of influence strategies we may be considering.

Should Christians use psychological techniques to influence people toward faith in Christ? The answer is a cautious yes, provided we correctly understand our own role in the context of God's total purposes. Then we will gladly make ourselves accountable to the Holy Spirit's prompting and the counsel of fellow believers.

In our discussions on this topic, we have been assuming that social influence is real and powerful. Let us now step back to examine the evidence that this is so.

Vulnerable to Influence

We do not like to think of ourselves as being easily persuaded. We each aspire to be independent of others' influence, making up our own minds and acting accordingly. How vulnerable are we to the influence of those around us?

In the early 1950s, Solomon Asch conducted several experiments on conformity to social pressure (Asch 1952). He asked people in a group situation to respond orally to a series of visual judgments. In each case, a line whose length matched a target line was to be selected. Unknown to participants in these studies, the other people announcing their answers were accomplices of the experimenter, paid to play a predetermined role. On several trials, they agreed together on the incorrect answer. The effects were dramatic: More than two-thirds of Asch's true subjects agreed with the majority vote, even though it was obviously wrong.

An equally powerful demonstration of social influence was reported by Stanley Milgram (1963), who studied patterns of obedience to an authority figure. Milgram asked ordinary citizens who had agreed to participate in a learning experiment to deliver electric shocks to fellow participants. Under the experimenter's urging, 60 percent of the participants complied by pushing the buttons to give high-voltage shocks to innocent persons (the shocks were never actually received). Milgram's research reminds us of the power others wield in influencing our behavior.

These two studies agree with dozens of others in pointing toward an uncomfortable conclusion: *We are much less independent than we like to think.* How does this conclusion compare with principles found in Scripture?

One dramatic illustration comes immediately to mind—Peter's denial of Jesus. As recorded in Mark's Gospel (14:29–31, 66–72), Peter confidently affirmed his loyalty to Christ. Even when Jesus warned him specifically of the upcoming events, Peter insisted that he would rather die than disown his Lord. Interestingly, Peter was not alone in this. Though their loyalty was never put to the test in the same way, the other disciples echoed Peter's confident boast. History has recorded the sad fact of Peter's blatant denial. Although we often regard him as a person of weak will, any of the disciples or any of us might have done the same thing.

Throughout Scripture, the truth of our vulnerability to the influence of those around us is both explicitly affirmed and implicitly assumed. The Israelites were warned to drive out all the godless inhabitants of Canaan lest these nations exert a corrupting influence, resulting in God's judgment on his people (Num. 33:55–56). The first chapter of Proverbs contains strong warnings not to go along with the urging of those who want us to join them in their violence and crime. Throughout this collection of practical wisdom, admonitions about the destructive influence of godless individuals abound (Prov. 14:7; 22:24; 24:1). The positive impact of associating with morally upright people is affirmed as well (Prov. 13:20).

The New Testament echoes a similar theme. Jesus warned his disciples to be on guard against the teaching and the influence of the religious teachers of their day (Matt. 16:5–12). Paul advised the Corinthian believers not to associate with immoral people who claim to be Christians (1 Cor. 5:9–11). Similar advice is applied with regard to any who are idle and who do not live by the clear teaching of God (2 Thess. 3:6–7). Paul also stated emphatically, "Do not be misled: Bad company corrupts good character" (1 Cor. 15:33).

In a remarkable way, both Scripture and social psychological research converge on the conclusion that those we associate with have a powerful influence on our behavior. Though the root of sinful action is found deep within the human heart (Matt. 15:19–20), the social environment cannot be ignored. To attempt to do so is simply to deny a dimension of our humanness.

How then can Christians living daily in a fallen world cope with the constant pressure to conform to the values and lifestyle of the surrounding culture (Rom. 12:2)? An inner transformation of the heart and the indwelling power of the Holy Spirit are essential for every believer who desires to walk with God. But there is more. We can choose to associate with those whose influence will be constructive. The Bible knows nothing of a *lone ranger* brand of Christianity. Every believer is adopted into the family of God (Eph. 1:5), becoming a member of the body of Christ (1 Cor. 12:12–13). As Bolt and Myers (1984) remind us, we live and serve in community, not in isolation. The disciple-making strategies of both Jesus and Paul bear this out. We are explicitly instructed to continue meeting together and encouraging one another (Heb. 10:25). We can be assured that God knows us thoroughly, including our need for social support and positive influence.

Having examined some of the evidence that our social environment influences us in significant ways, we now consider the interplay between faith and action, between belief and behavior. Once again, we will find biblical and psychological evidence in close harmony.

Belief or Behavior: Which Comes First?

It is commonly assumed that our attitudes or beliefs have a powerful impact on what we do—our overt behavior. For example, we expect that people's religious beliefs will cause them to act in a moral and altruistic way. Likewise, we are not surprised when those with known racial prejudice or anti-Christian biases display discrimination in their interactions with members of these groups.

A parallel theological principle is also widely accepted—namely, that faith in God is the source of obedient action. We generally infer that a person who steps out in faith to do something difficult or costly has a strong faith in God. While it is no doubt true that attitudes affect behavior and that faith stimulates corresponding action, this is only half the story. Social psychologist David Myers puts it succinctly: "We are as likely to act ourselves into a way of thinking as to think ourselves into action: we are as likely to believe in what we have stood up for as to stand up for what we believe" (Myers 1987, 130). Apparently, the causal chain works in both directions.

Throughout Scripture, the concepts of faith and action are closely intertwined. Abraham's faith in God led him to respond in active obedience, even to the point of being ready to sacrifice his son Isaac (Gen. 22:12). Similarly, Elijah was able to challenge the prophets of Baal on Mount Carmel (1 Kings 18) because of his conviction that Jehovah was the only true God. All the heroes of faith included in Hebrews 11—Noah, Moses, Rahab, and dozens of others—demonstrated their faith in obedient action.

Another perspective needs to be included as well. In James 2, both Abraham and Rahab are cited as examples of those whose obedient action led to justification before God. In fact, James makes it clear that real faith cannot exist without corresponding works to validate it. Consider also that when Jesus called his disciples, he asked them to respond with public action—stepping out and following him. While their response indicated that they believed in him, taking this action no doubt helped to strengthen an uncertain faith.

When we survey the evidence from psychological research, we find a similar pattern. Our attitudes do influence behavior, particularly when our beliefs are brought to mind before the choice is made. For example, if you are reminded just before voting that you strongly dislike lawyers, you will likely support a candidate with some other occupation. As well, the impact of attitudes is strongest when external constraints and social influences are minimal. You are not likely to act in full consistency with your beliefs when someone is holding a gun to your head!

Once again, however, there is ample evidence that actions impact our beliefs. If we harm an innocent person, we are inclined to disparage this victim; however, having done a favor for someone, we tend to like that person more as a result. When we continue to play a role that is initially foreign to us, we find the role becoming more comfortable and closer to our true feelings. Taking action to support a social or a political cause almost invariably makes us believe more strongly in what we have acted on. Without question, actions both shape and reveal our attitudes.

The principle of *cognitive dissonance* is often invoked to account for the link between action and belief. When we behave in a way that does not match our current attitudes, a discrepancy is created, and we are motivated to reduce the gap. This can be accomplished either by excusing the action as not representative of us—something we often do when coerced into action—or by adjusting our attitudes so they line up with the action. Recent evidence (Griffin and Buehler 1993) suggests that the change in attitude that results from discrepant action is probably based on a reinterpretation of the situation. In addition, they argue that this reinterpretation follows rather than precedes the action. In part, it is a matter of rationalizing an unjustified course of action.

We can best understand the relationship between faith and action or attitudes and behavior in terms of an upward spiral in which attitudes and actions continually reinforce each other (Myers 1987). This truth has relevance for both theological and psychological applications. A weak faith that prompts cautious, uncertain steps of obedience is strengthened in the process, resulting in both stronger faith and more consistent discipleship. Similarly, when a tentative liking of another person stimulates small and cautious acts of kindness or generosity, these actions make the attraction grow. Soon, the feeling is stronger and the acts of friendship are more significant. Which one appears to be the cause of the other depends on the point at which we break into the upward spiral of attitudes and actions.

Myers and Jeeves (1987) suggest several important ways in which these principles can be put to work in our churches and homes. New believers and new members should be encouraged to become actively involved in study groups and avenues of service as soon as possible. To wait for evidence of strong commitment is to delay the growth of that commitment. In worship situations, people should have the opportunity to act on their beliefs. A liturgy that has parishioners responding actively and verbally is preferred over one that leaves them as spectators. If it can be arranged, having people step forward to receive communion is probably better than serving them where they sit. Finally, the rituals that accompany special religious celebrations are not to be neglected. The Advent wreath at Christmas, special prayers on Thanksgiving day, and the family breakfast before Easter sunrise service have value in building the faith of Christians of all ages.

The significant role that outward actions play in confirming and building solid inner commitment should not be overlooked. In fact, the whole idea of separating what we know in our minds from how we live is foreign to biblical teaching. In all of Paul's letters, right living and right belief are closely linked. Jesus himself declared, "If anyone chooses to do God's will, he will find out whether my teaching comes from God or whether I speak on my own" (John 7:17). This is a profound truth. It is only as we commit ourselves to following God's purposes for us that we can truly know him.

Reflecting Back

In this chapter dealing with major topics in social psychology, the central concept has been **influence**. God has designed us to live in relationship not only with him but also with other people. Therefore, we are continually involved in social interactions with those around us, including family members and close friends, casual acquaintances, and total strangers. These interactions revolve around our influencing others, as well as our being influenced by them.

We explored the possibilities of social influence, seeking to determine whether or not the techniques uncovered by psychologists should be put to work by Christians in their efforts to influence others. While a variety of these techniques have proven effective, we noted the need for caution in their use, since ultimately, it is God's job rather than ours to change other people.

In two other areas, we noted a harmony between biblical teachings and psychological evidence. Research strongly suggests that our feeling of independence is largely illusory: We are vulnerable to the influence of both authority figures and peers. This conclusion matches with Scripture, in which we are frequently warned to be careful about whom we associate with. Finally, we explored the intriguing reciprocal relationship between observable behaviors and inner attitudes. There is good evidence from both psychology and Scripture that each builds the other. Beliefs and behaviors are practically inseparable.

Going Deeper

1. For a revealing discussion of the incredible power David Koresh wielded over his followers, read *Inside the Cult* by Marc Breault and Martin King (Signet, 1993).
2. For a good review of psychological principles of influence, I recommend chapters 6 to 9 of *The Human Connection: How People Change People* by Martin Bolt and David Myers (InterVarsity, 1984).
3. For a comparison of biblical and social psychological principles, consult "Yin and Yang in psychological research and Christian belief" by David Myers, *Perspectives on Science and Christian Faith* 39 (1987): 128–39.
4. For a brief and readable discussion of the interplay between attitudes and behavior, I recommend chapter 27 in David Myers's and Malcolm Jeeves's *Psychology Through the Eyes of Faith* (Harper and Row, 1987).

Epilogue

The Pacific Northwest offers a rich variety of both comfortable walking trails and more challenging hikes. When you go on a hike, it is good to look behind you from time to time in order to see where you have come from. The same applies to the journey of analysis we have taken in this book. Our terrain has been both varied and challenging; we have become acquainted with a range of topics and perspectives in psychology. Now it's time to look back.

Review of Topics and Themes

Topics considered in the various chapters have been linked to a central idea, one for each chapter. These key words have been **diversity, complexity, windows, awareness, behavior change, information, needs, growth, person, isolation, wholeness,** and **influence**. Now we can see the bigger picture, identifying several broad themes to which many of the topics in psychology are linked.

One such theme involves *personhood and relationships*. As unique persons, each reflecting God's creative design and skill, we find meaning in our relationships with others. We have considered the need for compassionate relationships when individuals suffer traumatic brain damage. We explored modeling as a powerful means of learning based on interactions with others. When death strikes, we grieve because significant relationships are abruptly broken. In professional counseling, the most important element is the relationship between therapist and client. Powerful impact on our values and behavior comes through the social influence of people around us.

A second theme resides in the "two handfuls of pinkish-grey matter" (Jones 1981, 13) that make up the *human brain*. We have seen that our brains play a crucial role in practically every action, thought, or sensation we ever experience. Certainly, brain injuries have profound implications for our daily lives. Our senses provide useful information about the external world only as our brains interpret these inputs. Dreams are accompanied by particular brain-wave patterns, and may even result directly from the activity of our neurons. Many human motivations are closely linked with brain functioning. Likewise, mental illness is often caused by abnormal brain activity. Some forms of therapy involve interventions in the physical brain. Clearly, the brain's role in human experiences of all kinds is vital.

A final theme evident throughout the topics we have considered is mankind's *dual nature*—our God-imaging and our fallen dimensions. In considering approaches that psychologists adopt in their study of human experience, we noted that some focus on our positive potential, while others emphasize our human frailties. Though our physical senses are often similar to those of animals, our understanding of what they convey goes far beyond that of lower organisms. In the topic of artificial intelligence, we saw both the creative human mind and the potential for our efforts to go awry. We noted that anger can be a terribly destructive emotion, but when it is channelled properly and expressed responsibly, it can help build deeper human relationships. It is impossible to look at people without seeing evidence of both sides of their natures.

In addition to pondering the themes that we have explored, I hope you will leave these pages with a firm conviction about the truth of several basic affirmations. These include the following:

1. The Bible is a rich source of insight, intensely relevant in our attempts to understand human nature and experience.

2. Psychology is a fascinating field of study, one that is rich in its diversity.
3. Differences in perspective are not harmful, provided we are willing to listen and to learn from one another.
4. When we attempt to relate Christian faith and psychological insights, points of both tension and agreement are found. The two fields are neither entirely compatible nor totally in opposition.

The Rest of Your Journey

In *The Opening of the Christian Mind*, David Gill laments the fact that we do too little thinking—that God's people are often "intellectually secular Christians" (1989, 41). What does he mean? Frequently, we make Christ Lord of our devotional lives and perhaps even our interpersonal relationships, but not Lord of our intellectual lives—our minds. We fail to love God with our whole beings, including our minds, as Jesus commanded (Mark 12:30).

In the Book of Proverbs, Solomon declares, "The fear of the LORD is the beginning of wisdom" (Prov. 9:10). Our understanding of psychology must be based not only on the observations of scientists and researchers, but also on a fundamental reverence for God and a thoughtful study of Scripture. Given the vastness of psychology and the depth of wisdom contained in God's Word, we face a great challenge indeed. This book is intended to propel you on your own journey of discovery.

As we part company and you travel on alone, I leave you with two suggestions. First, make a habit of regularly reading books and articles to stimulate the development of Christian perspectives on any and all issues you encounter. I have listed a number of helpful sources you can start with. Ask your professors for additional suggestions, or consult your local Christian book store.

My second suggestion is that you interact and discuss ideas with others who share your commitment to making Christ Lord of your entire being, including your mind. God has called us into membership in a community of believers; we need one another for both stimulation and accountability. Discuss what you are learning with fellow students and friends. Join a Bible study group or a book club. Keep a record of the insights you gain as you read and reflect, and bounce these ideas off other people. Take a course or attend a seminar on Christian perspectives in your area of interest. Get involved in community efforts that will challenge you to think hard about what it means to be a Christian in contemporary society.

The task of developing a Christian mind in psychology is a lifelong pursuit. For me, the challenge continues to be both rewarding and exciting. I hope you agree.

Going Deeper

1. For help in developing Christian perspectives in various areas of study, I recommend *The Opening of the Christian Mind* by David Gill (InterVarsity, 1989).
2. For better understanding of the purpose of Christian higher education, read *The Idea of a Christian College*, rev. ed. by Arthur Holmes (Eerdmans, 1987).

References

Adams, J. E. 1971. *Competent to counsel*. Grand Rapids: Baker.
———. 1986. *The biblical view of self-esteem, self-love, self-image*. Eugene, Ore.: Harvest House.
Allen, R. B. 1984. *The majesty of man: The dignity of being human*. Portland, Ore.: Multnomah.
Asch, S. E. 1952. *Social psychology*. Englewood Cliffs, N.J.: Prentice Hall.
Aycock, D., and S. Noaker. 1985. A comparison of self-esteem levels in evangelical Christian and general populations. *Journal of Psychology and Theology* 13: 199–208.
Bandura, A. 1977. *Social learning theory*. Englewood Cliffs, N.J.: Prentice Hall.
Beck, J., and J. Banks. 1992. Christian anti-psychology sentiment: Hints of an historical analogue. *Journal of Psychology and Theology* 20: 3–10.
Benner, D., and S. Palmer. 1986. Psychotherapy and Christian faith. In *Psychology and the Christian faith*, ed. S. Jones. Grand Rapids: Baker.
Bobgan, M., and D. Bobgan. 1979. *The psychological way/the spiritual way*. Minneapolis: Bethany.
———. 1984. *Hypnosis and the Christian*. Minneapolis: Bethany.
———. 1987. *Psychoheresy*. Santa Barbara, Calif.: Eastgate.
Bolt, M., and D. G. Myers. 1984. *The human connection: How people change people*. Downers Grove, Ill.: InterVarsity.
Brockner, J. 1988. *Self-esteem at work*. Lexington, Ken.: Lexington.
Bufford, R. 1981. *The human reflex: Behavioral psychology in biblical perspective*. New York: Harper and Row.
Clark, D. 1985. Philosophical reflections on self-worth and self-love. *Journal of Psychology and Theology* 13: 3–11.

Clouse, B. 1985. Moral reasoning and Christian faith. *Journal of Psychology and Theology* 13: 190–98.

Collins, G. 1972. *Fractured personalities*. Carol Stream, Ill.: Creation House.

———. 1988. *Can you trust psychology?* Downers Grove, Ill.: InterVarsity.

Coopersmith, S. 1967. *Antecedents of self-esteem*. San Francisco: Freeman.

Cosgrove, M. 1982. *B. F. Skinner's behaviorism: An analysis*. Grand Rapids: Zondervan.

Cosgrove, M., and J. Mallory. 1977. *Mental health: A Christian approach*. Grand Rapids: Zondervan.

Crenshaw, D. 1990. *Bereavement*. New York: Continuum.

Dobson, J. 1970. *Dare to discipline*. Wheaton, Ill.: Tyndale.

———. 1980. *Emotions: Can you trust them?* Toronto: Bantam.

Dreyfus, H. L., and S. E. Dreyfus. 1986. *Mind over machine*. New York: Free Press.

Emerson, A., and C. Forbes. 1989. *The invasion of the computer culture*. Downers Grove, Ill.: InterVarsity.

Faw, H. 1990. Does Scripture support standardized testing? *Perspectives on Science and Christian Faith* 42: 86–93.

Fowler, J. 1986. Faith and the structuring of meaning. In *Faith development and Fowler*, ed. C. Dykstra and S. Parks. Birmingham, Ala.: Religious Education Press.

Gazzaniga, M. 1988. *Mind matters: How mind and brain interact to create our conscious lives*. Boston: Houghton Mifflin.

Gill, D. 1989. *The opening of the Christian mind*. Downers Grove, Ill.: InterVarsity.

Gilligan, C. 1982. *In a different voice: Psychological theory and women's development*. Cambridge: Harvard University Press.

Gregory, R. 1990. *Eye and brain*. 4th ed. Princeton, N.J.: Princeton University Press.

Griffin, D., and R. Buehler. 1993. Role of construal processes in conformity and dissent. *Journal of Personality and Social Psychology* 65: 657–69.

Grounds, V. 1976. *Emotional problems and the gospel*. Grand Rapids: Zondervan.

Harlow, H. F. 1973. *Learning to love*. New York: Ballentine.

Hart, A. 1979. *Feeling free*. Old Tappan, N.J.: Revell.

Hendricks, L. 1989. *Discovering your biblical dream heritage*. San Jose, Calif.: Resource Publications.

Holmes, A. 1983. *Contours of a world view*. Grand Rapids: Eerdmans.

Hunt, D. 1987. *Beyond seduction*. Eugene, Ore.: Harvest House.

Izard, C. 1991. *The psychology of emotions*. New York: Plenum.

Jackson, E. N. 1980. Grief is normal. In *Death and dying: Opposing viewpoints*, ed. D. L. Bender and R. C. Hagen. St. Paul, Minn.: Greenhaven.

Johnson, C. 1983. *The psychology of biblical interpretation*. Grand Rapids: Zondervan.

Jones, G. 1981. *Our fragile brains*. Downers Grove, Ill.: InterVarsity.

Jones, S., ed. 1986. *Psychology and the Christian faith*. Grand Rapids: Baker.

Kelly, W. L. 1991. *Psychology of the unconscious*. Buffalo, N.Y.: Prometheus.

Kelsey, M. 1991. *God, dreams and revelations: A Christian interpretation of dreams*. Minneapolis: Augsburg Fortress.

Kohlberg, L. 1981. *The philosophy of moral development: Essays on moral development*. Vol. 1. San Francisco: Harper and Row.

Kohn, A. 1993. *Punished by rewards*. Boston: Houghton Mifflin.

Kouri, M. K. 1991. *Keys to dealing with the loss of a loved one*. Hauppauge, N.Y.: Barron's Educational Services.

Krych, M. 1992. Faith and cognitive development. In *Christian perspectives on human development*, ed. L. Aden, D. G. Benner, and J. H. Ellens. Grand Rapids: Baker.

Kübler-Ross, E. 1969. *On death and dying*. New York: Macmillan.

LaHaye, T. 1966. *The spirit-controlled temperament*. Wheaton, Ill.: Tyndale.

Lara, A. 1992. Conspiracy of kindness. *Reader's Digest*, May, 109–10.

Lindquist, S. E. 1983. A rationale for psychological assessment of missionary candidates. *Journal of Psychology and Christianity* 2 (4): 10–14.

Mackay, D. 1980. *Brains, machines and persons*. Grand Rapids: Eerdmans.

Madow, L. 1988. *Guilt: How to recognize and cope with it*. Northvale, N.J.: Jason Aronson.

Maslow, A. 1968. *Toward a psychology of being*. New York: Van Nostrand Reinhold.

Matheson, G. 1979. Hypnotic aspects of religious experiences. *Journal of Psychology and Theology* 7: 13–21.

McDonald, H. D. 1986. Biblical teaching on personality. In *Psychology and the Christian faith*, ed. S. Jones. Grand Rapids: Baker.

McLemore, C. W. 1982. *The scandal of psychotherapy*. Wheaton, Ill.: Tyndale.

Meier, P., F. Minirth, F. Wichern, and D. Ratcliff. 1991. *Introduction to psychology and counselling*. Grand Rapids: Baker.

Milgram, S. 1963. Behavioral study of obedience. *Journal of Abnormal and Social Psychology* 67: 371–78.

Motet, D. 1978. Kohlberg's theory of moral development and the Christian faith. *Journal of Psychology and Theology* 6: 18–21.

Myers, D. G. 1987. Yin and Yang in psychological research and Christian belief. *Perspectives on Science and Christian Faith* 39: 128–39.

Myers, D. G., and M. Jeeves. 1987. *Psychology through the eyes of faith.* San Francisco: Harper and Row.

Narramore, B. 1984. *No condemnation.* Grand Rapids: Zondervan.

Page, S. 1989. The role of exorcism in clinical practice and pastoral care. *Journal of Psychology and Theology* 17: 121–31.

Reeve, J. 1992. *Understanding motivation and emotion.* Fort Worth, Tex.: Harcourt Brace Jovanovich.

Robbins, P. R. 1988. *The psychology of dreams.* Jefferson, N.C.: McFarland and Company.

Sall, M. J. 1976. Demon possession or psychopathology? A clinical differentiation. *Journal of Psychology and Theology* 4: 286–90.

Schuller, R. 1982. *Self-esteem, the new reformation.* Waco, Tex.: Word.

Seamands, D. A. 1985. *Healing of memories.* Wheaton, Ill.: Victor.

Shepperson, V. L. 1981. Paradox, parables and change: One approach to Christian hypnotherapy. *Journal of Psychology and Theology* 9: 3–11.

Sire, J. 1990. *Discipleship of the mind.* Downers Grove, Ill.: InterVarsity.

Southard, S. 1972. *Christians and mental health.* Nashville: Broadman.

Tournier, P. 1962. *Guilt and grace: A psychological study.* New York: Harper and Row.

Van Leeuwen, M. 1978. The behaviorist bandwagon and the body of Christ. *Crux* 14: 3–28.

———. 1985. *The person in psychology.* Grand Rapids: Eerdmans.

White, J. 1987. *Putting the soul back in psychology.* Downers Grove, Ill.: InterVarsity.

Worthington, E. L. 1982. *When someone asks for help.* Downers Grove, Ill.: InterVarsity.

Yancey, P. 1977. *Where is God when it hurts?* Grand Rapids: Zondervan.

Index

Techniques, psychological, 177–80, 186
Technology, 18, 91
  and brain control, 33, 39
Telepathy, 45
Temperaments, 129
Therapy, 62, 160–67, 171
Tolerance, 121
Total depravity, 135
Touch, 41–42, 43–44, 52–53
Tournier, Paul, 155
True guilt, 155
Truth, 16, 18–19, 20, 105

Unbelievers, and truth, 19
Unconditional positive regard, 161
Unconscious mind, 56, 132, 139–42, 154, 161

Values, 163–64
Van Leeuwen, Mary, 23, 40, 75, 83, 91, 96, 98, 136, 138, 143
Violence, 14, 80
Visions. *See* Dreams
Visual sense, 42–43

Watson, John, 56, 70, 86
Weber, Ernst, 42
Weber's Law, 42
White, John, 165, 169, 171
Wholeness, 171
Wolterstorff, Nicholas, 127
Women, moral development, 119
Worship, 185
Worthington, Everett, 160, 166, 172

Yancey, Philip, 52–53, 54